Reading into racism

Routledge Education Books

Advisory editor: John Eggleston
Professor of Education
University of Warwick

Reading into racism

Bias in children's literature and learning materials

Gillian Klein

ROUTLEDGE
London and New York

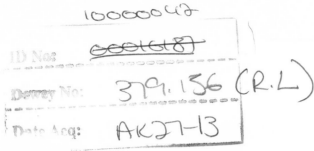

First published 1985 by Routledge & Kegan Paul Ltd
Reprinted 1986
Reprinted by Routledge 1990
11 New Fetter Lane, London EC4P 4EE

Transferred to Digital Printing 2003

Simultaneously published in the USA and Canada
by Routledge
a division of Routledge, Chapman and Hall, Inc.
29 West 35th Street, New York, NY 10001

British Library Cataloguing in Publication Data

Klein, Gillian
    Reading into racism: bias in children's literature
    and learning materials
    1. Racism in text-books
    I. Title
    370.19
    ISBN 0-415-05881-3

Library of Congress Cataloging in Publication Data

Klein, Gillian.
    Reading into racism.
    Bibliography: p.
    Includes index.
    1. Racism in text-books. 2. Text-book bias.
3. Children's literature. I. Title.
LB3045.64.K57 1985   371.3'2   85-8077
ISBN 0-415-05881-3

Contents

	Introduction	vii
1	What is a biased book? Recognition and responses	1
2	Negative bias – does it matter?	10
3	Oh, but *you're* different	30
4	Issues in fiction	44
5	Issues in World Studies	57
6	Bias in materials in other areas of the curriculum	75
7	The cumulative and the concealed: curriculum implications	92
8	Strategies for Combat I: Sanitize or sensitize?	108
9	Strategies for Combat II: Censorship or selection?	123
10	Conclusions: The watershed	141
	Bibliography	148
	Further reading	157
	List of organizations	159
	Author and citation index	161
	Subject index	164

To Leanne

*For whom books have
always been important*

Introduction

Prejudice in print is not new. Nor is concern about it, especially in relation to children. In the contemporary societies of Europe and North America, however, confronting the issues of racism leads to a new reappraisal of children's literature and learning materials.

This book identifies some of the forms that racism takes in literature and learning materials and illustrates ways in which the school curriculum may be affected and children's minds may be conditioned. It records some of the current approaches to racist materials for children and some of the strategies for combat that have proved effective. It describes initiatives by parents and communities, by teachers and librarians, by publishers and those working in the media, that actively challenge biased materials and raise the consciousness of children and those who work with them.

It is hoped that all who work with children or are training to do so will see the book as being directly relevant to the ways in which they use books and learning aids with children.

So many people have helped me to put this book together that I can only thank them all collectively here. My thanks also go to those on whose research and writing I have drawn freely, and who will find themselves acknowledged both in the text and in the list of recommended reading.

In recording the changes which may have resulted from these earlier writings I hope this book may itself be an instrument of further change.

I would like to thank Jessica Yates for pointing out a number of errors; I have taken the opportunity of this reprint to correct them.

Gillian Klein, September 1986

Chapter 1

What is a biased book?
Recognition and responses

> Mary Kingsley did more than study cannibals . . . she tried to
> change British ideas about the way Africans should be
> governed. She did a great deal towards securing justice for these
> backward races. (from *Reading On*, Red Book One. Oliver &
> Boyd. First published 1958, eleventh impression 1975.)

There is no such thing as an unbiased book. Every communication expresses the views of the individual or group of individuals making them. In the case of books (a word I shall from now on use to subsume other published materials such as cassettes, films, slides, videos, wallets of photographs, posters etc), those views are fixed in aspic for all who dip at any time in the future into that particular confection.

Much writing is candidly subjective: the author and the audience have both accepted subjectivity as being part – often a valued part – of the package. Writers like Buchi Emecheta or James Baldwin are actually exposing their subjective experiences and views, offering their vulnerability as a gift, a gift that at its best converts to insights on the part of their readers: 'yes, it's been like that for me, too' or 'now I can begin to understand how it must have been for them'. Great authors let us look out of their eyes as well as our own; how they see the world is a product of their own personalities, experiences and environments. Which is why Othello and Shylock are skilfully drawn stereotypes of other races as regarded by a sixteenth-century Englishman.

Works of literature

It is also why one position taken on the debate on literary bias is that

1

great literature is above or beyond such criticism. This is a position with which I would agree, though partly for a mundane reason: no one is likely to read Shakespeare at a stage when they have not developed their own views and also the ability to set what they are reading in the context of when and where it was written. Nevertheless, it is precisely when authors are writing with 'creative' subjectivity about groups other than their own that the anomalies creep in. 'Nice' black husbands for daughters of affluent American WASPs are handsome doctors, epitomized by Sidney Poitier in the film of the 1960s *Guess Who's Coming to Dinner*. When white authors set out to create black characters for whom they and their audience are intended to feel sympathy, they may judge them by white standards. Also, they often present them as victims, but victims of a system which is never questioned because, in the author's subjective view, the prevailing system is unquestionably acceptable.

Well-intentioned novels

For the well-meaning novels of the 1960s such as *Sounder* by William Armstrong, *The Cay* by Theodore Taylor, *The Slave Dancer* by Paula Fox, and Harper Lee's now-classic *To kill a Mockingbird*, the problem in all those works was identical. All the authors were white, and all were committed to creating in their novels black characters who would elicit their readers' sympathy and approval. The trap that all fell into was that they perceived their readers also as all white, and the ways in which they justified the worth of their characters were ways that would be wholly acceptable to white values and standards. But once articulate monitors of literature were being drawn partly from the black community too, it is little wonder that these finely-wrought novels drew fire.

In response, some white authors have been moved to seek a greater 'objectivity.'

Subjectivity v. objectivity

In itself, however, objectivity is not the solution any more than subjectivity is necessarily the problem. It depends on *whose* subjectivity and objectivity it is. And such a simple categorization leaves no space for the skills of empathy: Louise Fitzhugh, for example, immerses herself totally (and so her readers) in her central character in *Nobody's family is going to change*. That Fitzhugh was white and adult did not stop her creating in Emma a convincing, fat, middle-class Black American girl of twelve who is determined to become a lawyer. Emma is as real as *Edith Jackson* created by another fine American writer, Rosa Guy, who is black, and who acknowledges Edith as being closely modelled on her own life.

Works of creative imagination are necessarily complex, so simplisitic evaluations or conclusions will only impede debate. In their search for greater 'objectivity' authors may try writing collaboratively – which often means that they work with people who think and feel as they do: David Hicks and Simon Fisher, for example, when developing their *World Studies 8–13*, 1985 or the anonymous teachers who produced *Doing Things About the House*, published by Serawood House in 1983. Both works are honest attempts to communicate a particular view of the world: that it happens to be a benign, constructive view is what makes its bias so acceptable.

Another path pursued by would-be objective authors is a commitment to researching and then trying to impart a view less their own, but currently prevailing in society. This is where so many historians come unstuck. In 'boning up' the writings of earlier historians, they internalize and perpetuate the views and values of their source material – unless they make a deliberate effort to overturn them. Even working from contemporary documents – done so successfully by Tony Bayfield, for example, in documenting the rise of anti-semitism in Germany (*Churban – the murder of the Jews in Europe*) – is no foolproof guarantee: much of the material in *Churban* was actually used against the Jews and certainly there are authors like John Buchan and J.B. Priestley who read and accepted those or similar documents in precisely the way that they were intended, and then passed on their prejudice in their novels.

So objectivity is not only unobtainable; it is not necessarily even desirable. What needs to be identified when we look at the bias of the author is: *whose* bias is being reflected? One can find examples of black authors who have themselves so imbibed the prejudices of their own environment and education that they perpetuate it unquestioningly. In Sri Lanka in 1982, I was asked to look at a PhD thesis by a Singalese which argued that poor nutrition was the cause of low achievement *and intelligence* among Sri Lankans (both Singalese and Tamil). He was aghast when I said that the worthy tomes by British anthropologists of the 1930s, 1940s and 1950s to which he had gained grateful access at a characteristically colonial library in Colombo and on which all his argument was based, were almost bound to have been racist. This epitomizes the cause for concern. It is when the bias confirms in the reader a view of a group of people which is that of the dominant for the dominated, that bias becomes unacceptable.

Racist bias

We now move to a consideration of one form bias takes in books: racist. Many adults and children believe that books can be racist, and a consensus of opinion might offer this definition: 'a book that imprints a racist image on the reader's mind'. It thus becomes necessary to define what we mean in this context by *racist*. The racist view is that presented by the dominant (here, white) group of all other groups as being in some way inferior. The standards by which the dominant group measures all others are also themselves determined by the dominant group, so are inevitably distorted.

Racism in books can have many causes – from the unthinking and insensitive passing on of prevailing attitudes, to the conscious strategy of rendering the 'other' as 'lesser', in order to attack or exploit them. The most obvious illustration of the latter is the German propaganda that preceded genocide, rendering the Jews as 'untermenschen' – less-than-humans – such as the film made under the direction of Goebbels which cut quickly from rats eating corn in a barn to Jews at business (recorded in Bayfield).

Because we are here concerned mainly with English children's literature, it may be useful to examine at greater length the very similar process that sought to justify the exploitative patterns of colonialism. No one explains it better than Sivanandan and I recommend readers to study for themselves his exposition in *A Different hunger* (1982).

Where the dominated group are just simple, happy people in need of our paternalistic protection, we have justified the dominant group's behaviour. Beryl Banfield (in *Preiswerk*) illustrates how white Americans so justified slavery – from Edgar Allen Poe's faithful, contented – and stupid – slave in *The Gold Bug*:

> 'Oh my golly, Massa Will! Ain't dis here my lef' eye for sartin?' roared the terrified Jupiter, placing his hand upon his *right* organ of vision

through to Walter de la Mare's Sambo in his tale 'Sambo and the Snow Mountains'. Though this story first appeared nearly fifty years ago, it was published in Penguin's 1977 edition of *Collected stories for children* (1977).

This Sambo, third generation British despite the speech patterns given him by de la Mare, is just bright enough to know that if he were white, things would be better – and he not so slow and stupid. Which is why it took him 'exactly eight hours and a half in making up and learning this piteous rhyme':

A pill, a pill, is all he ask,
Dat take away his ink-black mask
And make him quicker at his task

Even a creature of Sambo's limitations can perceive that with a whitening-up would come a speeding up – and who of de la Mare's readers would have challenged this portrayal?

For there is an even more sinister effect of this kind of racism, one that has been identified by black philosophers and activists such as Frière, Fanon and du Bois. Luis Neves Falcon devotes a chapter to it in *The slant of the pen* (Prieswerk 1980). 'Through assertion, omission, concealment and mystification, the colonised people are forced to internalise as good the forces which are perpetually exploiting them.' He continues to stress the inter-relationship of children's books and colonialism: 'every dominating class has to develop, from among its very young, the cadres it will need to guarantee the preservation of its privileges . . . and to instil in them the ideological beliefs which give legitimation to its position of power'. And, conversely, there is a need to prepare the children of the dominated group for *their* position; children's books then become social tools by reflecting the values of the dominating classes. 'The printed word', Falcon observes, 'considered quasi-sacred in most dependent societies, in fact becomes a tool for transmitting to the children of dominated parentage the notion of their insufficiency and their natural inferiority.'

I expect that this is what happened to the Sri Lankan thesis writer.

Other forms of pejorative bias

The issues explored in this book are, as I have intimated, complex and interwoven, and one cannot let Falcon's observations pass without a recognition that the process he has so clearly described and related to racism is identical with the process which informs class prejudice. And because English writers for children are drawn almost exclusively from the middle class – and generally write for it, too – there is the parallel situation of working-class children and adults being portrayed by middle-class authors with a middle-class confidence in their own superiority. It takes an Alan Garner or Farrukh Dhondy to break the mould; a mould epitomized by Charles Kingsley or Rudyard Kipling who, writing in the nineteenth century, unquestioningly fixed their views for their readers. As did Charles Dickens, on both a conscious and an unconscious level; Steven Rose points out that, while the Artful Dodger talks in the language of the streets, Oliver Twist himself speaks impeccable standard English. Yet Oliver is no less a product of a workhouse upbringing; the difference is that his parents, and therefore his *class*, determined his upper-class speech patterns.

When we examine another area of bias: sexism, we are as likely to be reading a story written by a woman as a man. Women authors like Enid Blyton, Angela Brazil, Brett-Dyer put girls firmly in their place: it is interesting that Blyton, for one successful series, created a girl called George – a tomboy – for her young female readers who have not yet succumbed to the social pressures to identify with. Other women writers like Montgomery, Coolidge, Alcott, put on their pages even livelier – because better realized – 'heroines'. *Anne of Green Gables*, Katy of *What Katy Did* and Jo, the rebel among the *Little Women* leap gates and fly in the face of convention. They are all of an age to attract a readership in early adolescence – who may well, even if unconsciously, be looking for another way of growing into womanhood. These readers will be sorely betrayed by the authors: all these characters have their wings brutally clipped. To quote Marion Glastonbury, whose article 'What books tell girls' (see recommended reading) is definitive on this subject and a joy to read, 'If they don't end up *in* a wheelchair, they'll end up pushing one.'

Most of the examples in this book examine racial bias, but issues of sex and class bias cannot be ignored. They stem from precisely the same mismatch between the portrayer and the portrayed. I wondered why my daughter, an omnivorous reader, shunned John Christopher's excellently wrought science fiction novels that my less-enthusiastic-reader son fairly gobbled up: it took me some time to realize that my ten-year-old was already aware that she would grow up into a woman – and Christopher offers no women nor strong girls, only female ciphers (usually of extraordinary beauty). Maybe she missed an imaginative experience: luckily Jane Langton, (*The Diamond in the Window*) Antonia Barber (*The Ghosts*) and ultimately Ursula Le Guin were there to lead her into the realms of fantasy and help her to explore the unknown through the eyes of lively female characters.

Reading schemes

For negative examples of sex bias, one need look no further than the reading schemes, considered in detail in Chapter 6. And there are many other forms of bias that have not yet been mentioned – the aged as infirm, of unsound mind, or extraordinarily eccentric; the portrayal of the disabled – whether blind, lame or non-hearing; what they all need is the help of a ('normal') friend. Having considered some of the causes and forms of bias, the next chapter but one looks in detail at the most prevalent – and pernicious form – the pejorative stereotype.

Illustrations

Not only do words reflect bias – so too do the pictures in books. And they do it at the flick of a page, confirming an image in the mind or flashing a new one. Illustrations are considered in relation to the books examined throughout this study, but certain manifestations of bias in illustrations could usefully be identified here.

The best illustrators, like the best creative authors, draw realistic individuals and not stereotypes which means that members of ethnic minorities are based on individuals too. But artists of such skill and sensitivity are hard to come by, although their number is slowly growing. Some, like Errol Lloyd and Sharon Gordon are black and others like Bridget Hill and Lisa Kopper are white. It is publishers who need most to be alerted – although several who are, have been driven to despair. I remember the wail of one children's book editor: 'They all draw me SW3 children with black curly hair'. Rightly, she identified that white features, browned in, are as biased as grotesque caricatures.

Many series have based their material on photographs. This effectively avoids racial stereotyping but does not eliminate the possibility that the visual images in terms of *what* they portray, will be racist. When meeting a commission for the *Times Educational Supplement* (18 April 1980 – a contribution which the book editor saw fit to caption 'Peanuts to Tarzan') I submitted Marc Bernheim's *In Africa*, with a choice of possible illustrations to be used with the article carefully marked up: a doctor with a stethoscope, young boys on bicycles, a new housing development. But the one that appeared was of a woman pounding maize with a stick in a barrel, while a small boy, wearing nothing but underpants, looks on. Fine in the context of *In Africa*, which shows practically the whole gamut of

7

lifestyles on that vast continent, but a disastrous choice as the only picture to illustrate the piece.

Even illustrators who get the figures right may unwittingly be conferring stereotypes or stereotyped roles. However well the black woman is realized, she is only shown in a traditional housewife role or as a nurse, not driving (or mending) the car, or as a doctor. Other ways of portraying may require other ways of *seeing*: a new resource for schools by artist Natalie Ninvalle has sketches of, for example, a black judge, women with ladders, a bespectacled young black child at her steel pan – all possibilities for an extension of vision. And though it is aimed at the classroom (with the illustrations copyable and copyright-free) it could do much for children's book editors and illustrators.

Image and impact

The Schools Council study *Education for a multiracial society: curriculum and context 5–13* (1981) found and reported so much racism on the part of both teachers and pupils, that publication was very delayed. The report of the team makes clear that they considered books as powerfully feeding racist views. One team member, Mary Worrall, summed up the findings in an article in *New Era* (1980):

> When children of 9 to 10 years in different parts of England were recently given a free choice to fantasise on where they would like to go . . . Europe, America and the 'white' Commonwealth were overwhelmingly preferred. And when invited to write about somewhere they did not want to get landed in by mistake, they produced a narrow range of stereotype descriptions of jungles, 'primitive' natives brandishing spears, and dirty thin people. Africans, Indians and even Brazilian Indians were jumbled up in one confused notion of primitive, poor, uncivilised people . . .

The children were found to equate 'civilization' with guns and machinery or even sewing machines. When asked 'What things do you tend to think of when the word Africa is mentioned?' the answers could, Worrall reports, be 'summed up in one word: disasters'.

She follows through this image of the primitive, disaster-prone native, relating it to anti-black feeling, quoting from another team member, Rob Jeffcoate's example of one fifteen-year-old boy's piece on a 'modern problem' which concludes: '. . . when the war was on where were they then, they were all hiding in their mud huts. So I think the government should listen to Enoch Powell and get the immigrants out.'

Conclusions

Having in this chapter examined some of the origins as well as the manifestations of bias, it would be good to follow the thread and conclude where it ends. But an examination of the books in libraries, bookshops and those used in schools, suggests that the thread winds back upon itself, and could well continue to do so interminably.

The very children's books that originated in the era of Victorian paternalism are often, like Kipling and Dickens, still valued and read. This is due partly to their intrinsic quality, which makes them endure where newer stories are quickly forgotten. But it is due also to adults – be they teachers, aunts, grandparents – passing on to the next generation the books that enlivened their own childhood, without considering their relevance to today's young readers. These are adults who missed Joan Aiken's amazing Arabella, Alan Garner's *Owl Service*, Mildred Taylor's and William Mayne's very special worlds.

Contemporary authors could well bring to their offerings for children the characteristics, and even the values and opinions, imbibed from the books that delighted *them* as children. So are the biases of an authoritarian age perpetuated in many of the children's books in shops, homes, libraries and schools today.

Chapter 2

Negative bias – does it matter?

I sensed that a black skin invited images of a primitive world . . .
This image was fuelled by nearly every schoolbook available in
my schooldays that dealt with Africa. Mud huts, drums,
nakedness, savagery were, I felt, images of Africa and of black
people (in) many imaginations. I was petrified . . . I felt my
cover had been broken.

Keith Ajegbo
(from *Black life in a white world* in TLK no. 19)

Children's literature is a form of mass socialisation into language
and imagery as modes of representing the world and is probably
second only to television in its power as a medium of learning the
rules and expectations of society.

Phil Goodall (1982)

Subjective accounts, case studies and all the research suggest that
racism, sexism and other forms of negative bias in books matter a
great deal. There is, however, a view that *what* is in the books is no
longer important, as books themselves are nowadays irrelevant to
children.

As children grow older they read less. Media such as TV, films,
cassettes, comics are a greater part of their lives. A recent study
suggests that many children spend more hours in front of the
television than they do in school. And is information technology not
about to replace the book forever?

The role of children's books

If we look, however, at how books – and journals – are used, it soon

10

becomes clear that even though there are many other influences on children, the book itself has not been replaced, nor will it be during the school-days of the present generation. It continues to be the main medium of information for students of all ages and paves the way through the education system to higher study. Each time a student uses a book to find out or check an item of knowledge, the importance and authority of the printed world is also being reinforced.

Books are also being kept alive as the medium of imaginative experience and private delight – never more so than now. There is an impressive literature on the value of books in children's development, of which Bruno Bettelheim, Nicholas Tucker and Margaret Meek represent the pyschological and the academic approaches.

Then there are the professional initiatives directed at bringing more books to more children – the library strategies of radicals like Janet Hill (see her *Children are people*) who reorganized the library service of an entire borough, or the Bradford Bus, with its library, book shop, adult literacy unit, storytelling and Citizens' Advice Bureau all driving out to the community in one vehicle. There is the work done by those established bodies, UKRA, the National Book League, and the Children's Book Groups. Children's authors themselves do a good deal individually to keep the love of books flourishing, and work willingly with those other interested parties, the publishers, through Bookworm, Puffin clubs, and the Children's Book Circle.

Parental involvement

There are also parents' initiatives – Anne Wood was the first, and her journal *Books for Your Children* is still going, after eleven years. Harmony, an organization for cross-race families and also essentially a parent group, regularly reviews and promotes books they consider appropriate for children, as do many black parents' groups and women's groups.

Excitingly, these initiatives are no longer confined to the middle classes, as they were in the 1960s. Community parents' groups are also choosing and using books with their children. There may be outside support in the shape of a community centre/bookshop like Centerprise in London, or as school or LEA involvement, such as PACT (Parents, Children, Teachers). This movement was spearheaded by the Family Cooperation in Early Literacy Project, based at ILEA's Centre for Urban Educational Studies in the late-1970s. One thing that it did was to prove and document what was until then known by the parents, but not by the teachers of their children or by the authorities, namely: that *all* parents, however financially hardpressed, single, illiterate or non-English-speaking themselves, are eager that their children should learn to read. Not only eager, but willing to take an active role in assisting their children. What the Project – and its now widespread descendants – offered parents was ideas and information on ways in which they *could* help – by listening to their children read, by turning the pages of a picture-book together and talking about it, by involving older siblings to read to the five-year-old . . . It also offered books: loan collections were made available to the parents, who discussed how each had been received by the children, as they exchanged and selected the books at group meetings, their confidence visibly growing. The accessibility of books was maintained when the project itself ran out of funds, by the establishment in the children's schools or bookshops, run largely by the parents. These were among the first bookshops in primary schools, but their value has been known in secondary schools for two decades both by those with educational and those with commercial interests.

Other school-based initiatives have had an impact on children's reading although, as in the Bradford Book Flood experiment (Ingham) they may have been only short-lived. What no documentation can show is how strongly some of the children involved in such concentrated endeavours become lastingly 'hooked on books'.

Literature and culture

Many cultures employ a rich oral tradition for shared imaginative experiences. But for at least a century, British culture has relied on books for this purpose. Folk-tales are read aloud rather than told and contemporary writers create their own lasting legends. In this fixed and finite form, the characters and tales were bequeathed to children all over the British Empire and many are the children who are intimately familiar with Winnie-the-Pooh but have never seen snow or a gorsebush. Middle-class adults from Britain and the areas she colonized can find a common shared childhood acquaintance in Alice or Cinderella, Captain Hook or Ratty. This rich heritage of literature is seen as the birthright of all English-speaking children, wherever they may be. And this concept is built on and reconfirmed by modern children's writers, be they brilliant or banal.

For those children who do read for pleasure, as for adults, fiction is a magic carpet. It allows them a chosen, private journey at the most appropriate moment in their lives. Stories can transport us in space – to lands or lifestyles of which we could never be physically part. They can transport us in time, offering us all the wisdom of hindsight and bringing the past to life. Or we can explore the future, in the form of a tale based on a premise: it is this genre, obliquely related to myth and legend, which helps us to understand ourselves. And our understanding of the world can grow from the glimpses books allow us of that same world – through different eyes.

Identification

As a school librarian I observed that any child to whom literacy was not a problem, would read. The 'reluctant readers' much loved by those writers of 'high-low' stock cupboard fillers, simply disappear, if children who can read have the right book at the right time. Or if the child finds it for themselves. And the children seek out particular books at particular times of their lives: the most obvious is the inevitable attraction to novels about girls aged about fifteen by girls of twelve and thirteen (as Beverly Cleary knew, and Judy Blume now exploits to the full).

But *why* children identify with particular books at particular times is another highly complex issue – age and sex are certainly factors, and while there was never a time when we gave a book to a black child because it was about black characters, there is certainly evidence that black children pounce on such books. Especially when they are examining their own 'identity'. What John Tomlinson of Birley school points out always occurred, but was previously called 'adolescence' – black children acknowledging their colour as part of it. But children identify with the characters in their chosen books for all kinds of reasons, as all those creators of anthropomorphic Toads, Rabbits and Bears well know! While possibly labouring this point, I would like to emphasize another: whatever their reason for selecting a particular story book, children only read it to the end if it in some way satisfies them. Perhaps only their curiosity – in every good story one should want to see what happens next. But sometimes something much deeper occurs and what they take from the book, they keep. It is this unquestioning and total acceptance by the reader that we should keep in mind, particularly when, as in a library, no one is there to act as a buffer between the child and the messages of the book.

Research on children's reading

Research into whether and how children are affected by the messages in books has been prolific and wholly positive. There is far too much to review here: I shall mention only the most comprehensive, recent or startling.

There is no way of measuring the influences – qualitatively – on the human mind. Frank Whitehead and his team came nearest to determining what children took from their reading in a three-year Schools Council Project, *Children and their books* (1977). Whitehead looked at a sample of 8,000 children, and tabulated how many books each had read, and what they were (or, at any event, what the children said they had read!) His study makes illuminating reading, but what concerns us here is one of his conclusions. We can be reassured that reading *Rapunzel* to six-year-olds will not leave them climbing up each others' hair: children soon know that a story is only a story, and have no confusion about where the fiction ends. But what they do absorb unquestioningly is 'the values and attitudes of the author'. And it is these values and attitudes, the study concludes, that form a 'residue' in the child's mind.

A residue builds up and packs down, layer upon layer, and there are many of us in Britain who, with or without the help of race awareness training, are painfully scraping away at the residues so deposited in our own minds. These are residues that determine how we regard people of the other sex, other races, classes or age groups.

Racism is damaging to the perpetrator as well as to the target. Research in the early 1970s looked mainly at books in relation to the targets, the most extensive being that of David Milner, documented in *Children and race* (Penguin 1975 O/P). His tests showed white children as having a good self-image, while the majority (80 per cent initially) of the children of West Indian origin had a poor one. This was at a time when many schools, to judge from the pictures and self-portraits of the pupils, had no children in them who did not see themselves – or at least portray themselves – as white: advisers and inspectors speak with shock of the mismatch between the all-white art work and the ethnic and racial heterogenity of the population of many schools. Yet even in 1983, in ALTARF's broadcast on BBC2 *Racism – the 4th R*, a mother speaks of her nine-year-old, whose home has always consciously endorsed her colour, as rejecting a sundress because it exposed 'too much of this rubbishy brown colour'.

Milner set out to prove in that study that books and the media *do* matter and *can* effect changes in how children see themselves. He set up a two year 'multiracial classroom' for half his sample (with, of course, the control in an Anglocentric classroom). It had teachers, where possible, from ethnic minorities, and visits from other members of these minorities. There was also all the available literature and books – not a great deal in 1972 – that had children from ethnic minorities as central characters and adults too, in significant roles to which children could aspire. And *Little Black Sambo*, Noddy and his persecuting golliwogs, were out.

In two years, there was a change. Not in the control group, nor among the white children in the 'multi-racial classroom', but among those very children whose self-image was apparently so poor. About half the children of West Indian origin now felt more positive about their blackness. Again, it would be misleading to oversimplify: there were other significant factors operating, especially in relation to teacher expectation, for Bernard Coard's seminal book *How the West Indian Child is made educationally subnormal in the British school system* had already been published.

It is no accident that *Children and race* was not reprinted, because many things change, and one of these, which affected children, was the growth of an articulate black voice in the UK that located the problems in the right place – in the racism of the host society, and not in black people and their children. But there was an interrelationship between books and people here too: black people celebrated their blackness in print; works by African poets and writers like O p'Bitek were published in the UK, more fiction and picture books began to depict Britain as a multi-cultural and multi-ethnic society, and more of them did it sensitively, not just in a tokenist way. So radically did patterns change in the decade, that *Children and Race 10 years on* (1983) is much more than a second edition; nearly half the material is new, and it makes enlightening and edifying reading.

The Milner debate needs the counterpoint of the research at the University of Maryland in 1974, (unpublished) when the US was much further along in awareness of black identity. Again the sample was of five-year-olds, but all were black. The variable here was reading schemes: one group was invited to learn to read from *Dick and Jane*, a US equivalent of *Janet and John*, and indeed almost indistinguishable. The other was given material and supportive picture books that depicted black children in a range of activities and situations – and rapidly learned to read. Their performance exceeded the 'standard' for acquisition of initial literacy. Whereas the first group, totally unmotivated because they saw no relevance

15

in the 'treasure' of an all-white reading scheme, simply did not trouble to work for the key that would unlock it. No poor self-image on the part of these five-year-olds – but possibly a lasting poor regard for books. Until our educational objectives include producing well-adjusted illiterates, we do well to take account of this research.

Recommendations on racism in materials

Current documents do take account of research. The Rampton Report (1981) summarizes its views on books and materials as follows:

> Teachers should examine critically the text books and teaching materials they use and take account of their appropriateness to today's multi-cultural society.
>
> LEA's, through their advisory services, should help teachers to keep under review the text books and teaching materials they use and, as resources allow, provide for the replacement of those which display a negative cultural bias.
>
> Public and school librarians should attempt to ensure their stocks represent in a balanced manner the range of cultures present in British society, by including books which reflect the culture and achievements of West Indians and the contribution which they and other ethnic minorities have made and are making to this society and to other countries.

This is further underpinned by the Home Affairs Committee's Report on *Racial Disadvantage* (July 1981).

Such thinking has filtered into the Local Education Authorities and schools, so that many of the LEA Policy Documents on multi-cultural education invite a consideration of the resources used in schools. In ILEA's *Education for a multi-ethnic society*, for example, the questions on resources, while stressing that it is positive materials that need to be identified and used, ask also that criteria be developed for 'looking at materials to see to what extent they offer a stereotyped view of cultural and racial groups and contain negative and damaging content'.

There is a body of excellent literature that identifies negative bias in books for children and argues that these materials give offence and can be hurtful at worst, misleading at best. Details can be found in the reading list of the work of Dixon, Glastonbury, Kuya, Stones, Banfield and the CIBC, Zimet and Hoffman, Gill and Wright,

Worrall, Hedge and Davies. These writings will be referred to in the context of the curriculum area on which each author has focused.

Criteria for selecting materials

Some consensus of opinion has developed about what makes a book negatively biased and this has led to the development of criteria by which those who bring books to children, can evaluate the books in those terms and for racist and sexist bias in particular. The most comprehensive of these to be published in the UK was produced by the World Council of Churches, appearing in 1980 in their publication *The Slant of the Pen*. It addresses teachers, librarians, parents and also publishers and writers: the objective is to alert adults to the bias in existing children's literature and to discourage the production of new vehicles of bias. 'Racism', it states, 'hinders both sides from a fully human experience. The victims, dominant or dominated, cannot have a normal relationship with themselves or with others. Racism destroys both parties: it dehumanizes.'

Other criteria were published specifically with teachers in mind, such as ILEA's *Assessing children's books in a multiethnic society*, the CRE's *Checklist against racism and sexism*, the NUT's *In black and white*, and my 'Children's books, what to look for' in *Resources for multicultural education: an introduction*. All these criteria set out to heighten consciousness; it is doubtful whether any, and I can speak with certainty of my own, set out to be rigid yardsticks by which one selects or discards books. But the task was considered important: the first draft of the ILEA paper found its way into the *Tankits*, an early ALTARF initiative; the later version was extensively quoted in David Hicks' *Minorities* (1981) and in Richard Willey's publication for the Schools Council: *Multicultural teaching: the way forward*. The first issue of *Children's Book Bulletin* republished in full the World Council of Churches' guidelines, and all the guidelines referred to have a way of appearing, often unacknowledged and in a very pallid form, at courses for teachers and librarians.

It may be helpful at this point to set out, in tabular form, some criteria for selection which I originally published in *Resources for Multicultural education* (Reprinted 1984).

1   Select books which aim at a world view. Avoid books which equate the white man with 'civilisation', those with patriarchal or white philanthropical approaches to other peoples, or which

17

reduce all non-western societies to the exotic, the primitive or the quaint. These views may be evident in both what is said and what is not said: omissions can be equally damaging.

2 Select books that are factually accurate and up-to-date – the maps and illustrations as well as the text.

3 Select books which present peoples with a variety of attributes, whether of personal characteristics or life-styles; not those where whole cultural groups or individuals are portrayed as stereotypes ('the attribution of supposed characteristics of the whole group to all its members' David Milner, (1975), *Children and Race*)

4 Select books which use language with care: do Africans live in homes or in huts; are they ruled by kings or by chiefs; do they jabber and shriek; do they speak a language or merely a dialect; are whole peoples ever described as 'childlike' or 'savage'?

5 Select books that give students information about a variety of · cultures and societies, showing their effectiveness and achievements, whether historic or present-day. *Discovering Africa's Past* by Basil Davidson (Longman, 1978), for example, clearly illustrates that there were important and stable civilisations in Africa long before it was 'discovered' by the Europeans.

6 Select books that could equally well be used 'in an all-black classroom and an all-white classroom', and those which 'would not give pain to even one black child' (from Rae Alexander in *Interracial books for children*, Autumn 1970).

7 Select books which show children of different cultures and races carrying out the activities illustrated, be it in mathematics, design and technology, the sciences, music, etc.

8 Teachers of world studies and economics can be guided by the publications of the World Studies Project and paper by David Hicks, *Images of the World* (available from the London University Institute of Education). Each culture has its own values, and it is by these that it should be judged. 'Poverty' should not be defined as merely a lack of western goods. The reasons for the poverty of certain nations should be set in the historical and political context.

9 Science teachers should be on guard against any assumptions in textbooks that it is scientifically viable to classify people in terms of race. This type of classification can lead to the implication that one 'race' is biologically superior to others. See: *Race, intelligence and IQ*, a booklet from the National

Union of Teachers and *Bias in biology books: some points to look for* by Sue Watts (from Room 465, County Hall, London SE1).

10 Many religious education teachers acknowledge a special responsibility to avoid the approach that there is only one true doctrine. R.E. teachers are well placed to demonstrate that all religions provide a moral and social framework. The article by W. Owen Cole in *Education 3–13* (Autumn 1981) recommends some useful resources.

11 Teachers of English could consider their classroom books in terms of the fiction criteria outlined under personal reading. One possible approach is to consider the recommended syllabuses suggested by Scilla Alvarado (in No. 3 of the *English magazine*) representing Afro-Caribbean, Asian and black American authors at all levels up to GCE A level.

12 Reading schemes need scrutiny. If they show only white middle-class girls (helping mum) and white middle-class boys (kicking footballs) they are likely to be quite irrelevant to many of the children in the class.

Developing skills of evaluating materials for children

What seems more valuable is the way in which some groups have taken consideration of the issues a stage further. Bedford NAME for example, set up in 1979 a working party composed of teachers and children's librarians, to look at – mainly – racism in books. While they took into account the published guidelines, they ultimately developed their own. They did so in the light of the negative materials that they were evaluating together, and their knowledge and experience of how children might react in the schools. Thus the assessment skills of each member of that NAME group were developed, and taken back into the library service and the individual schools. Recently, Dudley NAME repeated the exercise.

There are schools around the country with working parties, generally focusing around the library (which might otherwise be left out if only curriculum materials were under review) that are re-evaluating the school's resources in terms of racism and sexism. Often they are part of a wider school or LEA initiative on anti-racism or anti-sexism. But the process of re-examining, and challenging, the printed resources is the same. So is the process of identifying the potential impact of bias on those who use the resources. In all cases, it is implicitly agreed that the books do matter.

Library services

It will come as no surprise that books are considered of great importance by librarians. Many children's librarians dedicate their work to imbuing in their clientele an abiding love of books. They, too, are eager that books should not hurt or mislead, and an increasing number are working with the support of their professional organization, and with teachers, to develop strategies for alerting colleagues to biased books and for combating that bias.

Two librarians who began to respond to the mismatch between ethnic minority readers and the books that were available in Britain in the 1970s were Janet Hill and Judith Elkin. Both saw their professional contribution, at that early stage, as best directed to identifying – both for their co-professionals and for the readers themselves – the few materials around that were even partly appropriate. The two resulting publications each served a dual purpose. Primarily, they offered the first bibliographic information on children's books that took account of racial and cultural diversity. But they also highlighted the dearth of material available, and the inadequacy of much of even those listed: indeed, Janet Hill's team graded a depressing number of materials as having: 'negative characteristics'. They continue: (these) 'whether bias, prejudice, inaccuracy, or dullness, outweigh all other considerations. They add nothing to understanding . . . and in many cases could be positively harmful'.

They, among others, have contributed to improving supply and creating demand, and certainly Judith Elkin had far more to choose from in her 1983 series of six articles for the journal *Books for Keeps*: 'Multicultural books for children'. But she recognizes, too, that the case for children's books in the context of the multi-cultural society still needs arguing.

> I believe that books have a vital part to play in a child's
> developing awareness and understanding. Books can foster
> racial and cultural understanding and offer children positive role
> models . . . Books can demonstrate the values of different
> cultures but also show the similarities between children playing,
> learning and growing up anywhere . . .

She also argues that books that give the impression that all significant characters are European are 'seriously misleading their readers' and will mislead even more powerfully where there are no classmates or evidence in community and High Street, to disprove this impression.

Increasingly, librarians are accepting their responsibility to provide materials that do not mislead their younger readers. Many are facing up to the fact that they can no longer continue to be 'restricted to the educated and literate part of the population' (Jaswinder Gundara 1981). Nor can the librarian maintain a 'value-free' or professionally detached position. The public library, despite its original purpose of serving the common people, 'has gradually moved towards providing a service to those most able to exploit its resources'. This needs to be actively reversed, argues Dr Gundara (brother of librarian Jaswinder); in fact it is the 'information needy' – the inner city population – who need to know their rights, the isolated, the unemployed and the non-English speakers, and those developing their literacy. And, he points out, 'libraries continue to stock vast amounts of materials which perpetuate unfortunate myths, stereotypes and prejudices'. (1983)

And an increasing number are doing so. What has not been acted upon is the recommendation of the Library Association and CRC (1976) that 'there should be a multicultural component in the training of all new staff, and in multiracial areas in-service training should be available'. This lack is seriously challenged by Ziggy Alexander (1982).

Library selection

For the present, the best library strategies are built round support: many Shire and County library services provide a comprehensive consultative display of current children's books (generally those published within the last two years), encourage teachers and others to examine each book before ordering it, and frequently augment the expertise they offer in advising this clientele with sensitivity to issues of bias. In some cases – it certainly operates in Leicestershire and Nottinghamshire – pasted into every book are one or even two reviews, and these reviews usually identify negative bias. This consciousness has been achieved by a permeation of the principles by which the children's and youth libraries operate. The reviewers themselves receive guidance on the criteria by which they judge each book, and in all cases attention is drawn to the need for accuracy, and to the unacceptability of pejorative stereotypes.

In ILEA, which provides a professional advisory team for the librarians working in schools and colleges and also supports the primary library post-holders (teachers), issues of bias are considered in all selection and training, the ILEA *Assessment paper* is freely disseminated, short exhibitions illustrating sexism or racism in books appear in the central libraries, and the most perniciously biased books are neither available from the loan collection nor present in the vast multi-media resource collection that is used for reference and for pre-purchase review.

Again it might be useful to set out some criteria for library selection also reprinted from *Resources for Multicultural Education* (1984).

Librarians should aim for a book stock which offers to children and young people:

1 A balanced view of the world, seen from many different perspectives.

2 Books which relate experiences common to children of all ethnic groups and in which they can all share, for example, the wobbling of that first baby tooth in *Berron's tooth* by Joan Solomon (Hamish Hamilton, 1978).

3 Books among which children from the variety of ethnic groups represented in Britain today can find characters which will confirm their own sense of self and enhance their self-esteem; in which ethnic minority characters have important social roles; where adults are seen to be supportive in family relationships and to hold positions of responsibility, doctors as well as orderlies, where ethnic minority children are seen to make their own decisions.

4 Books which communicate vividly and perceptively how it feels to be a member of another ethnic or cultural group.

5 Books in which black characters do not have to justify their blackness to the white characters (or readers) by being unbelievably good, or brave, or strong.

6 Books in which illustrations of ethnic minority characters are accurate and avoid caricature by using sensitive artists or photographs of real individuals.

7 Books which accurately reflect the population of Britain – so that those with an urban setting show not just a 'token black' (prevalent in publications of the 1970s), but represent cities and towns as truly multicultural – for example, Methuen's Terraced House series or *Mother Goose comes to Cable Street* by Rosemary Stones and Andrew Mann (Kestel, 1978).

8 Books in which language does not evoke stereotypes (avoid books in which 'savages' 'jabber and shriek' or the 'brown boy's eyes roll'); in which dialect is used appropriately – to extend expression and contribute to children's respect for one another's

speech – as in James Berry's or Linton Kwese Johnson's poems,
Charles Keeping's *Cockney ding-dong* (Kestrel, 1975),
C. Everard Palmer's *Baba and Mr Big* (Collins, 1976).

The book stock should also include folk tales which can bridge
cultures, and books written by young people, themselves from a
variety of cultures.

Reviews of new publications

General reviews of new publications for children also increasingly
take negative bias into account. These reviews are not just in the
likes of *Spare Rib* or *Multicultural Teaching* whose concerns would
guarantee such an approach, not only *Children's Book Bulletin* and
Dragon's Teeth which, like the American CIBC journal, are devoted to the social implications of children's books, but also to some
extent the *Primary Education Review* and *Secondary Education* of
the National Union of Teachers, the *School Librarian* under its
review editor, Margaret Meek and, belatedly but increasingly, the
Times Educational Supplement, Junior and *Child Education*, and
the ephemeral lists of current recommendations put out by libraries.

Children's responses to bias

Whether the bias in books matters to the children themselves invites
a multiplicity of views. Every initiative described so far is based on
an *adult* view that bias can be damaging, but some evidence is
emerging that some children are reacting against bias too. Mostly
with guidance from adults – several of these initiatives are discussed
in the chapters on combating bias.

When we look at the responses of individuals, be they children or
adults, we have moved out of the realms of research. What follows
could be given an academic legitimacy as 'case study', but I see it as
an extension of literature itself: an account of the experience of one
individual that may make us see the world, fleetingly, through that
individual's eyes. I believe the following accounts to be important to
our assessment of the significance of bias in children's books.

Consider, first, seven-year-old Maria who made *me* see children's
books in a new light. Her mother told me that Maria was sitting with
her book on her knee and a pencil in her hand, marking: 'This is
racist . . . this is sexist . . .' My first thought was that Maria was

23

unlikely to be getting much joy from her reading at present. But my second, more considered thoughts, brought me up sharply. What Maria was doing was what all children should be able to do – to challenge what they read, and locate the misrepresentations firmly on the printed page, where they belong. But there are certain things that helped Maria along; first, her mother and her teachers had taught her to trust her own judgment before that of some children's author; second, Maria, being black, could identify at a glance what she knew *from her own experience* to be distorted or untrue.

What, then, about my own son – who is white? Even had I instilled in him the same capacity to trust his own knowledge and experience about that enshrined in print (and I am not sure I had), what in that experience, the experience of a white middle-class boy, would have shown up for him the biases Maria so readily recognized? In reading that same book, was it not much more likely that the negative messages would simply have been taken on unquestioningly? Confirming attitudes already developing from the media, from his peer group, from authoritative adults in his life . . . contributing to the 'residue' in his mind?

Early reading is believing

Reflecting further, my mind went back to incidents some years previously when that same boy had just reached the miraculous click-point of being able to decode all the print around him. Like so many children when they reach that moment, he was reading everything – aloud. So when we found ourselves behind a van he read to me the legend 'Family butcher'. I thought that phrase might itself need some explaining, but before I could do so, the van doors opened and there hung all the carcasses. The next day we were travelling by Underground and again he brought his new skill to bear: 'It says "Way Out" there'. And together we followed the sign to surface at the street.

Growing up is about learning to operate independently in the (highly sophisticated) world, and what he had done was to use his new skill to make further sense of his world. He would now be protected by the 'Poison, not to be taken' on the tube of ointment; he would (probably!) avoid areas marked 'Danger'; he would, for a while, stay in that part of the swimming pool marked 'Shallow End'. And the reason was simple: not only could he now read but he believed what he read. He believed that the printed word would protect and guide him, and he would come to put his faith in telephone directories, road maps, newspapers and, of course, books. Nothing in his and his teachers' efforts to acquire that skill of reading had suggested that he should ever doubt the veracity of the printed word; in fact one of the ways he was helped to learn was by matching the print to the picture. The very process of learning to decode built into it a verification of that print. Much of the strategy for encouraging children to challenge bias in books must attack first the apparent inviolable authority of the printed word.

Confirmation or refutation

Add to all this the fact that my son at five, like all children, had already formed many of his attitudes with regard to race and to sex roles. Research by Davy, Goodman, Milner and others make it clear that these attitudes are manifesting themselves by the age of three, and may have formed earlier even than that.

Books are not going to overturn those attitudes at a stroke. But if they are not to confirm them, then they have to refute them. Those of us who are concerned with the education of children will have to recognize that if the curriculum – and that includes the hidden curriculum – and the resources in the school do not teach against bias of a negative or pejorative nature, then they are reinforcing that bias.

Painful messages in print

The remaining case studies all relate to people from the ethnic minorities and their encounters with bias in books. Dorothy Kuya describes movingly in her talks how, by the age of nine, she had still never seen a book about any people other than whites. Growing up in Liverpool and an avid reader (notwithstanding the literature) she stumbled at last upon a book all about a black boy. It was *Little Black Sambo*. Anyone who has heard the pain in Ms Kuya's voice when she speaks of this encounter will not be surprised by the position she took later in her contribution to *The Slant of the Pen* (1980):

> We must start writing new books . . . if we write about others, particularly those who have been and are still oppressed, we must first consult them. For the time being, it might be better if white writers stopped writing about things of which they have no

25

knowledge or understanding, and in humility made way for writers from those groups they have helped to oppress. But more than anything, we must ask ourselves if books are the best way of conveying information to our children.

The distress may even be public. Pictures of naked 'savages' such as those in the Penguin Primary Project (which Penguin has now withdrawn) or caricatures of cannibals with bones through their noses, have certainly been known to lead to sniggering and finger-pointing in the classroom, and hurt all the children, although in different ways and certainly in degree. A.F. Watts describes how his classmates, were 'reading and grinning and glancing round the room' in his short story: 'Integration, Northern style'.

We are reading Poe's *The Gold Bug* . . . Jupiter is afraid of the dead bug. None of the white fellows are afraid. Nobody's scared but Jupiter. He's rolling his eyeballs which are, of course, very white and talking like an ignoramus and murdering the King's English. Then there's this word 'nigger' that's going to be read out loud by somebody in just a few minutes. And there's me, the only one of me in the whole class . . . There must be at least two whole pages sprinkled with 'massa' and 'nigger'. When it comes to my turn to stand up and read . . . if I don't draw that same stupid part! Jupiter's part. The 'nigger' part! Me! (1976)

Black children in Britain have felt the same. It is enough to have to operate in a racist society without having literary respectability endorse the prevailing views.

Lest the familiar accusation of 'oversensitive' be levelled at this point, I shall let a black student who came to England from Jamaica speak for herself. This is taken from her essay 'My Schooling in England' which is published in *Education and the Afro-Caribbean Child* (1981):

My first real embarrassing moment came about in this same class. The teacher read a book called the 'Little Piccaninny' which I thought was ridiculous. It put across a picture of little black girls being really dim and stupid. She looked at me and said, 'We have a little Piccaninny in our class, haven't we?' I was very upset as I felt I was thought of as being stupid as this little girl. These sort of books are damaging to the black child and other children. This was the only black book I came across at school.

Language

There is strong reaction, too, against not just characters but even our 'Queen's English'. Dale Spender titled one of her books *Manmade Language* and in it she illustrates how the language makes half the world disappear. In terms like 'mankind', research has shown that 'man' does not 'embrace', but actually excludes women: 'Young children thought that man meant male people in sentences such as "man needs food" '. Or if it acknowledges women, it diminishes them by depriving them of 'semantic space': a 'female surgeon' or 'woman lawyer' signifies a departure from the norm, a norm occupied by the male; in less prestigious occupations, we have a 'waitress, a stewardess, a majorette.'

And a final case study, even though it has been printed often before, is Ossie Davis's study of Roget's *Thesaurus*:

> The word 'whiteness' has 134 synonyms, 44 of which are favourable and pleasing to contemplate. For example, 'purity', 'cleanness', 'immaculateness', 'bright', 'shiny', 'ivory', 'fair', 'blonde', 'stainless', 'clean', 'chaste', 'unblemished', 'unsullied', 'innocent', 'trustworthy', – and only ten synonyms of which I feel to have been negative and then only in the mildest sense such as 'glossover', 'whitewash', 'grey', 'wan', 'pale', 'ashen', etc.

> The word 'blackness' has 120 synonyms, 60 of which are distinctly unfavourable, and none of them even mildly positive. Among the offending 60 were such words as 'blot', 'blotch', 'smut', 'smudge', 'sullied', 'begrime', 'soot', 'becloud', 'obscure', 'dingy', 'murky', 'lowtoned', 'threatening', 'frowning', 'foreboding', 'forbidding', 'sinister', 'baneful', 'dismal', 'thundery', 'wicked', 'malignant', 'deadly', 'unclean', 'dirty', 'unwashed', 'foul', etc. In addition, and this is what really hurts, 20 of those words – I exclude the villainous 60 above – are related directly to race, such as 'Negro', 'Negress', 'nigger', 'darkey', 'blackamoor', etc.

Message versus muse

Strangely, there is one last and powerful group which believes that the messages in books, hence bias in books, matters to children, and that is the producers of those books. 'Strangely' because in November and December of 1980. David Caute orchestrated a spurious but nevertheless acrimonious debate in *New Statesman* of which he was then literary editor. He ranged on one side the 'creative' authors, represented by Jill Paton Walsh and John Rowe Townsend, and set them at the throats of 'social critics' Rosemary Stones and Marian Glastonbury (both authors themselves) who would, it was claimed, threaten their creative freedoms by campaigning against racism, sexism and class prejudice in children's books. There was one 'creative' author, Robert Leeson, claiming (with justification) that he could be creative *and* socially aware, but the battle is still hinged on an either/or position. It was as absurd as Tweedledum and Tweedledee, but the saucepans were banged until Ken Worpole's letter silenced them all:

> In the 1950's and 1960's when . . . writers were 'free' to write whatever they wanted unhampered by 'guidelines', what kind of books did they write? For the most part parochial, sentimental, unimaginative rubbish. In the 1970's, however, with the active interest in children's literature by feminists and committed teachers, writers were encouraged to stop and think before they set their wooden characters marching round their toy town plots . . .

If the 'creative' authors were indeed fighting for their professional autonomy, for their right to be biased, it did not mean that any of them were actually intending to write racist or sexist books. The odd thing is that children's authors and publishers still perceive their readership in much the same way as did the first authors of books for children in the early nineteenth century, those upholders of the most authoritarian and paternalistic era of all in Britain. That is, they perceive children as innocent, plastic, as having open minds to be worthily filled; as having malleable characters, still to be shaped. Today we may frown on *Struwwelpeter*, with its terrifying warnings of what may befall the erring child, but authors and publishers eagerly produce books on going to hospital, Mummy and Daddy get divorced or Tommy can't walk.

So, on the one hand we have the sanctimonious and parental, on the other, the creative muse struggling to loose the bonds of social constraint. Either way, the producers of books for children have assumed that the messages in them are very important indeed.

Conclusion

So while a blueprint would be an abomination, and no criteria can be definitive, there is good reason for the debate on bias in children's books to continue. Who reads what, when and how, acceptingly or questioningly, privately or as a prelude to classroom or family discussion – these are some of the considerations that determine whether or not the bias in any particular book is acceptable. But one all too familiar criterion, expressed recently in defence of *Little Black Sambo* by a teacher at an international conference, has totally outlived its usefulness, and it is this:

'I read that book as a girl – and it didn't hurt *me*.'

Chapter 3

Oh, but *you're* different

The forms that bias in children's books may take are as numerous and as various as the books themselves. This chapter does not attempt to analyse all these forms, nor even all the forms in which racism manifests itself.

A typology of racism in books does exist; it can be found in *The Slant of the Pen* (1980). Jorg Becker has identified seven patterns of argumentation by authors which will, alone or in combination, result in racist books.

Here we consider chiefly two of the most widespread forms of bias, generally described by the terms *omission* and *stereotyping*; some of the many other forms will most usefully be considered in the context of books on specific themes or subjects. But because they go across all media communications and because the terms have developed their own meanings for the campaigners against them, it seems advisable to examine omissions and stereotyping in some detail. When we then apply the terms to story books and curriculum materials we will be using them in a tightly defined way.

Omission

'Omission' is self-defining. The most dangerous aspect of omission is that books may very effectively conceal what is left out of them, or even that anything has been left out.

Most authors write with considerable conviction, carrying their readers with them. It takes some time before one can learn to step back, pause, and reflect 'Something is missing here'. Authors and editors determine what will be dealt with in any given book; if the reader cannot find what she wants there, she will be advised to seek out other books on the subject. But authors also bring to their writing their own perspective, and if their view is blinkered, so will their book be.

The subtlety of some forms of omission can hardly be overstated. Nor can their potential for informing the reader's view of the subject. Many popular novels and stories, of course, do it deliberately; we are told only what we need to know in order to be sure of who is good and who is bad and where our sympathies should lie. But the way material is selected for inclusion can even be unintentional; whether it is the *Dam Busters* one is reading, or practically any account of the heroic acts of, say, the British Air Force in World War II, or American cowboys – and even American Indians – there is never a mention that some of those brave fighters were black. Yet contemporary documents and many of the photographs now housed in the Imperial War Museum show individual black soldiers, and of course whole black and Indian battalions, who fought just as courageously on the 'good' side. William Loren Katz has published in the US a number of books based also on contemporary documents which relate the actions of black people in the pioneering West (often hilariously) and describe also the complete black Cavalry Corps who rode in to 'protect' settlers and enforce the law. Some of these regiments were so embittered by their racist treatment from the whites for whom they were risking their lives, that there is even a documented case of one group riding out to Mexico and shaking the dust of the US forever out of their horses' hooves. But how many children ever get to know these things?

Omission in books about other countries

There are misleading omissions in the way other countries are portrayed in books for British children, and these will mainly be dealt with in Chapter 5. Again, the reader needs to look carefully at what is put in, in order to realize what has been left out.

This is well illustrated by two rather useful and carefully wrought books on Africa. The one, *In Africa* by Marc Bernheim (Lutterworth 1974) is in my view an excellent example of a simple picture book which shows a wide range of lifestyles and conditions in a vast continent. It is still a necessary antidote to stories for young children which talk of people in 'Bongoland', who live in 'huts'. Yet among all the people portrayed by the Bernheims, in rural, village and urban environments, there is no Asian face to be seen. Which, considering the Aryan migrations and the colonial policies of indentured labour from India, is an omission indeed. *Zambia* in the Beans series (1979) is also subtly distorting: this time because the second sentence is already telling us that 'Her village has hot water for most of the year, and she and her brother Mulenga don't need shoes when they go to school.' Here it is not possible to pinpoint precisely what is missing. One is just left with the uncomfortable conviction that there are other items of information about Juleta that would be far more interesting and useful to know.

Obvious omissions

Omissions that are perfectly apparent are inevitably absurd. It takes only a page or two of *Children of the Cape* (Colbert, 1960) for example, before the omissions glare at us. The mix of pictures and text dwells on two 'Children of the Cape' – their glorious school set in the mountains (which they attend in impeccable uniforms), their capers on the equally glorious beach, their visit to a fruit-farm. They are, of course, white. We learn from this book that *all* children of the Cape are white. Admittedly, the book is old – it was in fact written at about the time that a six-year-old visitor to South Africa embarrassed me with the question: 'I see a lot of black Mummys and Daddys, but where are all the black babies?' That had to be answered with an explanation of apartheid, and children could well ask the same question about this book. Although it is as out-of-date in its style as it is distorting in its content, this book is still in use in a Midland school, a school, moreover, with an 80 per cent ethnic minority intake and with such a commitment to books and libraries that two teachers are fully timetabled to administer and teach in the library. The one I spoke to, who has responsibility for the library, told me that she 'had never seen a biased book'.

Omission and language

Looking again at *Children of the Cape*, it affords yet another example of omission, one that revolves around language. Not only are there no black children in the Cape, there are no black people. Certainly there are pictures of several, but these are never termed 'people': they are 'apple-pickers' or 'workers' in the vineyards – described for their function, not their humanity. They are here only to make life even more congenial for the white children – in fact, the 'apple-picker' is even equipped with a hand large enough to 'grasp the apple with the whole of his hand, so as not to bruise it. It is a great art and the coloured people make wonderful pickers'. But this demeaning of blacks into no more than a robot-like service agent for whites is another issue.

Omission and censorship

Omission will be considered again in subsequent chapters, but one further point is of a wider significance in terms of racism, so invites scrutiny here. In the debate on censorship – reviewed in Chapter 9 – it is acknowledged that the line between censorship and selection is exceedingly fine. As writers, editors and publishers select what information to put into their books, they inevitably select also – or censor – what to leave out.

Kuya (*op. cit.*) identifies this process as a vicious circle:

teachers, parents and others buy books to convey information to children because they conform with their knowledge and understanding . . . this information is then regurgitated in the classrooms of Britain. So our children grow up knowing nothing of the diversity of cultures and religions, within which there is a constant dynamic development; they are told nothing of the elements of life which go to make up an individual's or a group's existence. Nothing is said about the economic/political/social/religious/ideological framework within which all groups and nations operate. All they encounter are stereotypes, distortions, irrelevant information, misleading and ambiguous statements and downright lies – a reflection of the views which were common currency during the period of the British Empire: paternalistic, often contemptuous, bigoted and racist.

Omission of women

Women and girls may feature in fiction, but they are largely left out of history – unless they happened to be Queen Elizabeth or Florence Nightingale. They are, as we have already seen, largely left out of the language of 'mankind', or subsumed within it, so the argument goes – which comes to the same thing. In the same way, they are subsumed – or omitted – in accounts of past events, unless they happened to be in a position of power at the time. When one looks at *Ordinary Lives* by Carol Adams, one is confronted with a whole area of past lifestyles that is almost entirely new to the literature. There are women reloading their men's guns behind the laager in the South African textbooks on the Great Trek, but no others, either white or black, were ever acknowledged. These identified women were in an important subservient role, and the implications are of class bias as well as sex bias. There are whole areas of children's literature where women never appear – from the inevitable and numerous examples of science primers, to those which confirm the notion that 'man makes his world'.

There is a further body of literature which reduces women to the same organs of function as we saw with the treatment of black women and then in *Children of the Cape* and which takes no account of the working class except also as service ciphers. But this dehumanizing and diminishing can be considered as a function of stereotyping. Stereotyping is closely allied to omission.

Stereotyping

A workable definition of stereotyping appeared in Milner's 1975 edition of *Children and race*. It is 'the attribution of supposed characteristics of the whole group to all its individual members. Stereotyping has the effect of exaggerating the uniformity within a group, and its distinction from others.'

Stereotyping is not in itself destructive. In order to store information in those inadequate and quirky computers, our minds, we need to arrange and categorize it in such a way that new items of knowledge can be slotted into appropriate compartments. It is argued that our learning is based on stereotyping. Buckingham (1983) would argue that 'it is an inevitable aspect of human thought and representation.' If we know that a dog barks, we can assume that the sound of barking denotes a dog around – not an elephant.

This is acceptable as long as our assumptions are based on empirical evidence. Too often, however, they are based on an isolated experience. Or on images in books and the media. Or even on hearsay. And these stereotypes are formed by a consensus, a consensus based, as Perkins (1979) has illustrated, on the dominant ideology and power relations of the society, and so serving the dominant sector of that society. This is where the pejorative element comes in. Sandra Wallman explained it at a conference on Teaching about Prejudice in 1983, but her paper was not published in the resultant booklet, so I will give the essence of it here.

Identity versus Identification

It is the dichotomy between identity and identification that Wallman explains as being at the root of prejudice. And it is a prime cause of pejorative stereotyping. We are all content to be described in the way we choose to describe ourselves: too often, however, it is a view formed by others, dominant others, that forms the basis of the stereotype and is therefore likely to be disparaging. For if the dominant group is the norm, and inevitably its members so perceive themselves, then any other group is deviant – deviant along a spectrum from exotic and quaint to threatening, or inferior.

'The exception that proves the rule'

Such stereotyping does not assist in learning; indeed a prerequisite of learning about others may often necessitate unlearning the stereotype about them. For so powerfully does stereotyping preclude objective thought, that it is possible for people to hold two totally opposed stereotypes of one group of people in their minds at once, and believe both. West Indians, for example, come and take all our jobs, *and* are all lazy and on the dole. Jews are mean *and* they throw their money about ostentatiously. Further examples are given by Allport, cited above.

As with omission, one never gets the full picture. But here it is obscured by the residue in the mind. So fixed do these derogatory stereotypes become, that one can encounter literary or living evidence that totally refutes the stereotype, and deal with the mismatch without any of the discomfort of having to think again, to reassess. 'Oh, but he's different' . . . even 'the exception that proves the rule' leaves the structure of the individual's assumptions intact, while considering 'the exception' independently. Even with propaganda at its most powerful and virulent, creating in Europe in the 1930s and 1940s a stereotype of Jews that would permit their ultimate extermination, individual German and Poles effortlessly managed the necessary acrobatics of the doublethink. Himmler is recorded as complaining: ' . . . every Party members says, "Sure, it's in our programme, elimination of the Jews, annihilation – we'll take care of it". And then they all come trudging, eighty million worthy Germans and each one has his one decent Jew. Sure, the other are swine, but this one is an A-1 Jew'. (from Keneally, T: *Schindler's Ark* (1982).)

There were few individuals who applied their recognition of the merit of their Jewish 'friend' to challenge their stereotype of the entire race. Too few, at any event, for it to help Europe's Jews.

How we see ourselves

It is unlikely that any single book or media image would therefore explode the pejorative stereotypes held in children's (and adults') minds. But it is no part of education to confirm them. What educational resources can offer is a commitment to presenting to children other groups as they see themselves and such a wide variation of representatives of any group as to defy generalization.

Michael Storm, as Geography Inspector of ILEA, once in a talk pleaded for 'the endless extension of stereotypes', a strategy to be commended in that it will a least broaden children's views. But it seems to me that it is the inherent belief and feeling in us that we are the norm and that it is any difference from ourselves that we base our stereotype upon, that is at the root of this form of prejudice. So an effective strategy for attacking the construction or confirmation of stereotypes may be to teach similarities rather than differences.

Similarities rather than differences

Biologists will tell you that a Swede and a San, an Austrian and an Aborigine, are more alike physiologically than a sparrow and a robin. But while it harms no one to bunch the latter together as birds, it is the way we sort out the people of different races and living in different countries that develops our 'knowledge' about them along lines that lead inevitably to stereotyping. That all races are very alike, not only physically, but in terms of tneir drive for survival, their aspirations, their capacity to care for others, to work, play, hope and feel, is something that children would benefit from knowing. But it is not part of the curriculum – although the World Studies 8–13 Project, discussed in Chapter 5, does develop this thinking. Even if all schools adopted the curriculum of WSP it would be only a start: the thinking needs to be implicit in all learning and teaching, part of the hidden as well as the overt curriculum.

Role stereotyping

As well as stereotyping groups of people, children's books tend on the whole to uphold stereotyped roles for people. Anti-sexist studies such as Adam's *The Gender Trap* have identified with great clarity how women are locked by literature into stereotyped roles. It begins with the picture books, too numerous to cite, where only Mum does the cuddling – and the cooking – and Dad does all the 'work'. It continues in reading schemes: John climbs the tree while Jane is there only to watch and admire – before trotting off to help Mummy in the kitchen. Even the brave new world of *Breakthrough to Literacy* (MacKay *et. al.*, 1970) which sought to give a less stereotyped and less middle-class view of the world to beginning readers, shows adults, particularly parents, in stereotyped roles, and leaves most of the adventure to boys. *Breakthrough to Sexism* by Celia Burgess and *Radically revised reading schemes?* by Rose- mary Stones, provide valuable analyses of the depiction of women as only home-makers even though most women now also hold jobs outside of the home (and they hardly ever wear trousers, but frequently do wear aprons over their skirts), and of girls as either passive and domestic or, when they do get to climb the tree, confined to the lower branches!

Role stereotyping in terms of race, sex and class endorses the 'supremacy' of white males by ensuring that they are always in the positions of power. Blacks or working class characters are here to serve and maintain that supremacy – the fundamental flaw in novels like *The Cay*, or to be the beneficiaries of their philanthropy – starting with *Robinson Crusoe*, who saved Friday's soul, if not his life. How many stories are there where black characters are con- stantly supplicating or thanking whites for their kindnesses?

Role reversal

Anti-sexists have used a strategy of role reversal to combat role stereotyping. There are films like *Rosie the Riveter* and books like *Clever Gretchen and other forgotten folk tales* in which it is the Princess who does the rescuing. Fathers shop and cook while mothers go out to work. This device has a highly desirable effect on people with even the most hardened residues: it pulls them up sharply. There is something in that resource that does not fit comfortably with their views and attitudes, does not confirm, comfort, reassure. The predictable reaction will appear counter- productive: 'But that's not how things are. This book is nonsense'. It needs a parent, teacher or librarian to say that that *is* how things are even if only in a minority of cases, and that there is no reason why things could not be that way even more often. This role reversal is often intentionally amusing, it is always intentionally provocative: consider the word 'herstory'.

Upholding the stereotype

The difficulty for those combating role stereotyping or stereotyping of groups of people, is that there is often enough truth in the stereotype to confirm its validity. That is because it is built into the process: the role models put before girls in both life and literature is too often of women in subservient positions. These issues are taken further by Buckingham and others, and are quoted and considered in the chapters on combating bias.

White children will be more likely to aspire to the roles and positions which are held – indeed *reserved* in a society like that of Britain or the United States, where racism is institutionalized – by whites. Middle-class white children, seeing potential for achievement all around them and reflected in the media as being their province, are still statistically the ones who aim high. They certainly have not encountered enough role reversals to change their beliefs, assumptions and aspirations.

It is that perpetuation of 'the grain of truth' by the media and in society that makes stereotyping so destructive. Basically, people – child or adult – believe what they want to believe. They take from any experience or presentation of ideas and information only what fits most easily into their existing framework of knowledge and perceptions. It is easier to select from the external image that which appears appropriate, than to make a perilous and painful shift in our whole mental framework in order to accommodate a contrary notion.

Literature and the media therefore comfortably relate to the already fixed views and stereotypes of the dominant society, meeting their readers', listeners' and viewers' expectations almost all of the time. That is a 'common' viewpoint to which 'everyone' subscribes: a viewpoint which, in a racist and sexist society, is inevitably racist and sexist.

Exploiting the stereotype

There are groups of people who deliberately exploit this situation. National Front literature makes much of the fact that many Jews, like many other settlers, have worked industriously for the betterment of themselves and their families, and produce, in magazines for children like *Bulldog*, scurrilous series such as 'Billy the Yid'.

And though it may be seen by many to be innocuous, there are 'comedians' who make their living by delivering material that is based on a shared view of other groups – inevitably a derogatory one. Books often enshrine this particular form of bias, so it may be illuminating to consider here sexist and racist jokes.

'Jokes'

Most of the comedians are male, and the women who brought them into the world they exempt from the female stereotype. Instead, it is of 'the wife' or mother-in-law. She is simultaneously stupid and dominating, also avaricious, possessive, complaining and a bad driver. The laughs are raised because the audience accepts these stereotypes.

So it is with racist jokes. I hesitate to commit an example to print, as it has to my dismay aroused laughter in discussions about racist jokes, but one is needed. So, here it is, in the form of a riddle:

Q. 'Why are banknotes green?'
Answer No. 1 'Because the Jews pick them before they're ripe'
Answer No. 2 'Because the Irish pick them before they're ripe'

The two answers can be used interchangeably to get the laugh. It is interesting that the audience will be making a different assumption in each case, in order to understand the 'point' of the joke. Not that the Irish are so avaricious that they cannot wait for the money to ripen, nor that the Jews are so stupid that they cannot tell, but the other way round. And the 'humour' is enhanced by the whimsy that banknotes grow for the gathering.

No Jew, no Irish person, would be likely to tell that joke. They may tell jokes about their own people, but the required shared assumption among them would be quite different. Not necessarily all that benign: humour of this kind is often tinged with malice. But, for example:

'So these are your grandchildren' (to a Jewish woman) 'so tell me – how old are they?'
'The doctor's three and the lawyer's five'.

Racist, as distinct from racial, jokes are a device for keeping people in the place in which the dominant group want them kept. The

U.S.A. spawns floods of 'Pollack' and 'Puerto Rican' as well as anti-black and anti-semitic jokes. Britain is adding 'Paki' stories to their very extensive repertoire – the abuse terms are delivered lightly, as though with humour.

Cannibals

A singularly offensive genre of racist jokes is those concerning cannibals. So popular are they as a source of amusement, that Puffin devoted a whole section to them entitled 'Eatable People' in their joke book *The End* (indeed!) published in 1980. Wildly witty offerings like: 'Cannibal to air stewardess: "Don't show me the menu – just the passenger list" '. It was alarming to see in that same library-orientated multiracial Midland school in which the teacher-librarian had, as I have recorded, 'never seen a biased book,' *The End* going from one hot little hand to another.

It is beyond my ambition to delve into the psychology of this concept of cannibalism. Suffice it to make two points: (1) that cannibalism has been attributed by one group to another that they despise and/or fear in case after case (I even heard it said about Tamils in Sri Lanka in 1982) without any foundation whatever in fact; and (2) this concept of eating or being eaten causes a particular frisson among children, and is illustrated by their eager reception of *The terrible Nung Guama*, a Chinese folktale in which the monster threatens to gobble up the heroine, or the lasting popularity of *The three little pigs*.

In childen's eyes, it may be an incarnation of all the evils they most fear; it is an ultimate term of abuse, and no joke for anyone involved. As Katie, a middle-class girl at the middle-class birthday party of another seven-year-old discovered. She ran sobbing, to her mother reporting that the other children were calling her 'Cannon-ball'. Whether it was she or her persecutors that got the word wrong, Katie nevertheless recognized the jibe for what it was: a cruelly pejorative epithet that applied to her, and her alone – because she was the one black child present.

Golliwogs

Deemed equally 'harmless' by its perpetrators is that close relation to the cannibal; the golliwog. He, of course, wears clothes, and is often presented as a rather cuddly and endearing character. Though not always: Dixon's brilliant essay 'All things white and beautiful' (1976) argues that golliwogs are associated with fear and darkness, quoting an Enid Blyton tale of Noddy trapped and robbed of his car and his clothes, even his 'dear little hat' by 'four big strong golliwogs'. Dixon observes how a four-year-old got the message from the pictures alone, which show the golliwogs driving off and 'poor little' Noddy on the ground.

If he is not menacing, the golliwog is at best a diminished and ridiculous figure. Dressed in the servile minstrel apparel of that creation of the White South of the black man, used also by Bannerman to illustrate her Little Black Sambo of India, they are there simply to provide amusement to the whites. Recently, Brandreth had a little trouble convincing sensitized publishers that golliwogs are harmless. Five of them turned down his project before Pelham accepted and published *Here comes Golly* in 1979.

But here, in all his colourful glory, he came. Quite undamaged by the tactful amputation of the 'wog' from his name. Golly is greedy, Golly is stupid, Golly is a giggle. He eats his food so quickly that he gets the hiccups – and that is the whole story of this glossy publication. Another racial stereotype retained for children in the 1980s.

Reverend Basil Manning, who has done much work in racism awareness training, leant his support to a campaign against golliwogs in 1982. He wrote a letter to Boots – as a result of which and from the effort of other campaigners, the golliwog sponges were withdrawn from the market. This was the letter:

Dear Mr Ridley-Thompson,
As a black person who is deeply concerned about the subtle messages which perpetuate racism in British society, I thought it appropriate to write and share with you the following modern parable:
'There was once a director of a large company, a man concerned to please the community and especially thoughtful of the needs of children at Christmas.
One year he designed a product, easy to produce in large quantities, eye-catching and colourful. Children and parents up and down the land bought his "golliwog" sponges. Mothers and fathers taught their young children the word "golliwog", and thousands, maybe millions, of children were very happy that Christmas.
Some twenty years later the children who once happily played with their "golliwog" sponges one Christmas were now abusing black people in Deptford and the East End. "Go home wogs"

and "Wogs out" read the slogans on the walls and on the doors of black families who tried to clear their hallways, hearts and minds of the after-taste of excrement pushed through their letter-boxes. Everyone wondered where these young people had learnt these hateful sentiments.

The children who once enjoyed their "golliwog" sponges in their baths, now marched on the streets shouting slogans of hate; "Keep Britain white", "Niggers go home", "Wogs out". Then one day they killed an Asian in the East End, another day they beat up black people as they came out of a factory, months later another shot at a black man in Lewisham and still later some killed a man in Southall.

A new breed of racists from yesterday's children had been created.

The director was shocked by this state of affairs in his years of retirement and said, "I am not to blame. I always saw golliwogs as an innocent part of our folklore, besides, James Robertson used the same image for years on his marmalade labels, the nurseries used *Little Black Sambo*, people in their thousands went to the "Black and White Minstrel Show".

The teachers said: "We are not to blame that the only image of black people we had in reading books was that of a "golliwog", besides, the image of black people which we were brought up with was that of a caricature with wide eyes, red, thick lips and bright white teeth. We were not to blame for the media's omissions of giving only token reference to black people in positions of authority and responsibility".

Everyone said they were not to blame for the level of racism, the violence and disorder on the streets. Nobody accepted the blame not even the retired director. But the reality was that a new generation of racists was born, worse than their slave-trading and colonialist forebears, more deeply entrenched in racism built on that history of exploitation.

Some saw the light and made reference to the Nazis and the Germans who claimed they didn't know. And the children, now grown up said: "We have felt support for our ideas and actions – after all we started learning and thinking with products which bore the full stamp of approval . . . by appointment to Her Majesty the Queen".

And the director said: "Would that I could live my life again". But, alas it was too late for him, and for Britain.'

Others have made similar mistakes, can we learn from them?

Yours sincerely . . .

Accusations of 'over-reacting' to golliwogs can be met with this letter. It is only white people who 'see nothing wrong with golliwogs.' Black people recognize them as another demeaning stereotype, along with cannibals, minstrels and Aunt Jemima, created and perpetuated by the dominant group. And children's literature serves as a medium for their perpetuation.

While stereotyping may be dismissed as harmless, it is easily recognized. Omission is less easily identified. We have at all times to keep at the back of our minds 'is this the whole picture?' when we look at each individual publication and also at the collection of materials, be it a library or a set of curriculum resources. Both omission and stereotyping will be considered further, in relation to specific subject areas and as forms of pejorative bias which need to be combated.

Chapter 4

Issues in fiction

We have already considered the potential power of fiction to shape children's views and attitudes. We need also to keep in mind that fiction is not just that story that 3b is 'doing' or that is being read by teachers to the reception class. It is also the imaginative journey taken by the solitary child with her head in a book – in which she is guided by the author, and the author alone, and follows where the book leads. And it is the phrases and images that are left behind, either when that voyage has ended, or when the reader has opted out along the way because the book failed to hold her interest, which we cannot afford to ignore.

The history of prejudicial print in children's books is as old as the first children's book. It has been traced by Dorothy Kuya (Prieswerk 1980) right from the seventeenth-century: one of the first books for children was *The Adventure of Robinson Crusoe* by Daniel Defoe. She analyses how the 'social and cultural destruction' of the black man is based on the assumption of his inferiority. He is given a 'better' name, language and religion, his nakedness and cannibalism are corrected, and he is, appropriately for Defoe and his readers, so deeply grateful that he offers to his white 'master' his service and ultimately his life.

Subjugation of black characters

Certainly Defoe set a pattern for the portrayal of blacks in children's literature. If they were 'savage' or 'primitive' they were bad; if they served a white 'master' and accepted his definition of 'civilization', then they were 'good' – but still inferior. And, generally, helping white heroes of the ilk of Captain Biggles or James

Bond would cost them their (less valuable) lives.

Some authors even tried to explain their inferiority – the widely-read Willard Price, for example, comes up with this interesting statement based on the equation of virtue with education in *African Adventure* (1963, reissued 1971):

> Make no mistake about it – most Africans are kind and good.
> Every year more of them go to school. (He continues:)
> There are still millions of Africans who have never spent one
> day in school; without education, they still believe in strange
> things – that a leopard-man can turn into a leopard, that the
> heart of a strong man will make you strong if you eat it, and that
> no white man can be trusted.

Though history books are examined in Chapter 5, the attitude described above is often identical in information accounts, so could usefully be mentioned here. Black people in the areas colonized by the British who did not become servile, who did not acquiesce to their exploitation, like Chief Moshesho of the Matabele or Chaka of the Zulus are, like the American Indians, inevitably portrayed as 'savages'.

Once people are safely subjugated, the next form of racism is either to make them disappear completely, or to portray them as happy with their lot, since they are too simple and childlike to conduct their own affairs. A whole body of fiction embraced and expressed those views in the nineteenth and twentieth centuries – some, like the stories of Kipling, Rider Haggard and Charles Kingsley, have survived as classics. *Huckleberry Finn* too survives, but the controversy around it continues (see Inter-racial Books for Children Bulletin 1984) and though American schools are reluctant to ban this product of its time, it is increasingly being abandoned as a class set work.

A black academic, John H. Wallace, has adapted *Huckleberry Finn*, eliminating the offensive term 'nigger' and the portrayal of Jim as potentially dishonest and untrustworthy. Writing in *Washington Post* (1983), Wallace maintains that Twain's book maligns all black people and that this is particularly unacceptable in the U.S. where 'every black child is the victim of the history of his race in this country'. He describes how his own son lost enthusiasm in English classes after being asked to participate in the reading of *Huckleberry Finn* in an otherwise white class. Wallace reminds us that it was condemned upon publication by Ralph Waldo Emerson and Louisa May Alcott, among others, but is nevertheless now venerated in the States as 'classic'. Certainly, a study of the original with his adaptation alongside would be a useful exercise for both teachers and students alike.

American authors certainly did a consistent stereotyping and demeaning job on their servants and slaves. The house slaves portrayed in Margaret Mitchell's *Gone with the Wind* (1936) are widely known. They are either capable and caring servants whose only concern is for the well-being of 'superior'(!) white characters such as Scarlett, or they are devoted and dotty in the extreme, like the idiotic young maid.

Beryl Banfield has published a study of the white Americans' portrayal of slaves in literature, to be found in *The Slant of the Pen*, as 'ill-equipped to survive their own freedom', to which may be added 'and ill-equipped to strive for and attain that freedom'. These attitudes will also be considered in relation to the portrayal of people in history, in the following chapter.

Once the stereotype is established of a dependent and childlike people, it behoves the white characters in children's literature to be kind to them. *The Beautiful Chinese Take-Away Palace* (1980) illustrates this point: it should be said that I am not, in this study, offering the 'worst' examples of 'bad' books: I am more concerned to employ selected examples to illustrate each definable *form* racist bias may take. And it should also be said that the author of this example, Geraldine Kaye, is familiar with life and culture in Hong Kong, is sympathetic towards it, and has written a number of other books for western children in which her sympathy does not descend to patronizing pity.

But here she lurches over into the 'be-kind-to-the-poor-child,-it's-not-their-fault-they're-different' mode of racism, which inevitably implies that it may well be their fault. So we get the 'baddie' locals mocking Kai-Cheng's appearance and rhyming 'chinky' with 'stinky', and we get the 'good' English hero, Amy, protecting him from his classmates.

We also have Kai-Cheng a powerless victim, because all the English he knows is 'very good', 'yes, please' and 'no, please', 'very sorry', 'okay' and 'one Hong Kong dollar very cheap price', and so sure is Kaye that this litany is good for a giggle that she uses it over and over in her story. It is true that the author also points out the ignorance on the part of the teacher which adds to Kai-Cheng's misery, but it is only when *he* has the skills that allow him to correct her that matters can be put right. There is no suggestion that she should inform herself and maybe examine her own attitudes and, after all, as she smugly tells him, 'you are learning our ways at last' – no more living in a cupboard for our hero, he's one of us now!

Simple and simplistic stories

'High-low' or remedial readers, like reading schemes, are considered with curriculum materials in Chapter 6. But there is an
overlap into children's fiction that simplifies to such a degree that it
strips the characters down to the most basic stereotypes. It happens
with 'mums' too:

> 'Mum, Dad, this is Gerry . . .' I didn't even know his last name.
> 'Sanders. Pleased to meet you.'
> 'Gerry, these are my parents, Mr and Mrs Stein.'
> 'Would you like a glass of milk and a piece of fruit?' my mother
> asked. 'You're very thin.'
> 'Mom,' I interrupted, 'we haven't got time for snacks. Let's
> go.'
> (Rosenberg 1970) or:
> He goes into the living-room – they always call it the living-
> room because Dad says that is where they live, where Mum does
> the cooking, where they squabble over the washing-up . . .
> (Tate, 1980)
>
> or, from *The A–Z of Man* (1979) 'What's all this about Man?
> What about Woman? "Man" stands for the family of Man. Men,
> women and children are all "Man" '.

The parallel is with comic books. This is too big a field to deal with
in detail here, but Jenny Lashley's study (1972) is highly informative. I wish only to use the analogy with comics to illustrate how
oversimplification can lead to pejorative stereotyping. The artists
and the readers understand the conventions and assumptions that
make it possible to communicate in the simple form of the comic.
All schoolgirls, for example, will have identical features; readers
tell them apart by the length, colour and degree of curl of their hair.
Which serves well enough – until a Chinese or black character
appears. They are always drawn in the most racially stereotyped
way – and their only purpose for inclusion will be as an oddity, a
'baddie' or as a buffoon.

There are popular authors who use this comic-book shorthand
into the child's mind in much the same way. Blyton's schoolgirls are
equally interchangeable on the page – the only recognizable one
was Sophie – because of her stammer. Good for identification and
for a joke stereotype at one stroke. Blyton also stereotypes *all* her
adults – the 'normal' ones like parents are generally spirited away by
page 3, and reappear only to make cocoa at the very end and hear the

whole jolly story of what happened to their children. All other adults are either evil, eccentric or both. Bond and Biggles, themselves stereotypes of the intrepid blue-eyed empire builder, meet only with cardboard characters of the most stereotyped kind. Blacks are almost inevitably the enemy – the nearest they will come to a positive attribute is to be portrayed as cunning. The rare 'good' blacks are in the servile mould already described.

Women are either termagants or sex objects – again readers are referred to a more particular study by Rosemary Stones (1983). Mothers also have an exclusively servicing role in the cardboard style children's books. They are there only to comfort and cook – or possibly they represent the authority which the central character must defy, unless a stereotyped father is wheeled in for this role.

Parents are the first characters to round out and become human when portrayed by authors who realize their characters fully and introduce subtlety and complexity to their delineation. Most of the modern material referred to so far is of a facile and ephemeral nature – if it were replaced with something better, it would hardly be missed. The stereotyping is a function of its shallowness.

Substantial and enduring fiction

Modern children's books which may, like the classics, endure, are in another category and are given separate consideration in the following pages. It is the way that the characters fairly leap full-formed off the page that draws readers into the book. It may be fair to say that blatant stereotypes do not sit comfortably in such a fully realized world. Many of our best children's authors, Joan Aiken, Alan Garner, Peter Dickinson, Rosemary Sutcliff, Leon Garfield, Patricia Wrightson, William Mayne, Russell Hoban, Ursula Le Guin, to name but a fraction, bear this out. But this does not free them from bias – each world is that of the author's own creation, in some cases (like Hoban) quirkily individualistic, in others delineating a world that traps them into accepting the prejudices of the times, as Leon Garfield does in *Lucifer Wilkins* (1973), where the slave is a kind, gentle but also simple giant, who needs the sharp little cockney to tell him what to do next. Dickinson is so swept up in his Tibetan snowscape, that *Tulku* (1979) can be seen as both racist and sexist. Yet this is the author of *The Devil's Children* (1970, reprinted) the tale of a group of Sikhs trapped in Britain when the 'Changes' cause it to revert to medieval times, with all the parochialism and prejudice that poor communications and hard times bring. In this novel, one of a fine trilogy, Dickinson exposes prejudice; in *Tulku* he often merely expresses it.

Stories expressing prejudice

Bernard Ashley is also caught at times by the same biases that he sets out to expose. In *A Kind of Wild Justice* (1978) he leads his young readers into the underworld of the East End, indicates to them some of the pressures that make adults behave as they do, and draws his characters with a sharp and skilful pen. But the bias of our society comes through unchallenged in the final message of the book: being white, even if you are a snivelling illiterate nine-year-old, you may well survive on your wits, but if you are Asian, however honest, industrious and able you may be, there is no hope. I find this message, rather like that in some of Dhondy's stories in *East End at your Feet* (1978) that the only strategy for survival is to surrender your Asian culture and identity, dispiriting. Followed by discussion, these books can be recommended, but as private reading, whether by white or Asian young people, the message received may be: it is not good to be Asian.

Bernard Ashley's early novel is another case in point. *The Trouble with Donovan Croft* broke new ground when it was published in 1976. The trouble with Donovan was not that he was black (although Puffin sensitively changed the cover for their 1977 edition, as Oxford's original suggested that that might indeed be the problem). The trouble was that he was temporarily traumatized into silence by what he saw as his abandonment by his mother when she returned to nurse a dying parent in Jamaica, and by the fact that his father's shift work makes it necessary for him to be fostered.

Donovan's foster parents are experienced and compassionate. They are also white. They and his foster brothers care for him and even speak for him. And it is in response to his foster-brother's kindness that Donovan finally regains his speech, crying out a warning and so saving the white boy from being run over. Is there not a certain paternalistic bias operating here? And something of the black obligation to the white philanthropists? It is hard to say what overall message children will get from this book when they read it to themselves. What is certainly clear is the reason for its popularity as the first story that would introduce the issues for discussion to juniors. Third and fourth year classes who have worked through Donovan with teachers committed to raising the issue of racism as the first step to combating it, have found it immensely positive.

They are helped also by Ashley's sensitive care never to permit a racist statement to appear on his pages without its being instantly challenged and refuted. In fact, Donovan's foster mother is allowed to fly into a rage at the way he has been abused by the woman next door: She accuses her of 'ignorant prejudice' and tells her 'you make me ashamed to be white'.

But it is clear enough that the neighbour is racist, without her cat needing to be named 'Nigger'. For this is the language of racism, and does not require validation in print, nor to trip uncriticized off the tongues of ten-year-olds, because they have to read it aloud in class. Ashley won The Other Award for *Donovan Croft*, an award presented annually for new children's books of literary merit and which are also concerned to challenge class, sex and racial prejudice.

Sambo of 'seventy-seven

More clearcut is the story of 'Sambo and the Snow Mountains' in Penguin's 1977 *Collected Stories for Children*, by Walter de la Mare. Again the pejorative term, this time much in keeping with the mocking style of the whole story. The author's considerable genius with words is bent to amuse his readers (white?) by ridiculing a black child. We are no sooner told that Sambo's grandfather was a king in his own country than he assures us 'but it was a very small country'. Though Sambo's single great desire: to be white, must be self-explanatory to de la Mare's audience, he offers playful explanations: Sambo's uncomfortable thought about how black he must appear between the sheets on his bed for example, or his realization that 'without his night-shirt he could not be seen in the dark'.

More humour is wrought from Sambo's efforts to make himself white – not just his 'piteous rhyme' (already quoted on p. 5), but his indiscriminate swallowing of the physic he in desperation steals from his master; some of which 'made him giddy, or hot, or breathless, or limp, or excited, or silly, or talkative, or thirsty or hungry – or just the reverse; and one or two of them made him sick. After these his face looked a little green, but even then it was only a black green and soon passed away'.

A suitably absurd solution is found for Sambo: he falls into a tub of whitewash, and it is in this guise that he finds himself in the company of a grand old lady called Miss Bleech (sic). If there is anything left to say on the subject, de la Mare says it here through the persona of Miss Bleech: 'A black man whose mind is free from darkness and his heart from cruelty is in truth whiter than *any* one whose soul is in the shades.' One wonders why Penguin did not simply leave out this story, which first appeared in 1933. Yet the most recent reprint (1984) still regales black readers and white alike with this zealous fable in support of the merit of whiteness.

Desert island derision

Black people are degraded in a particularly pernicious way in another reissue, this time from 1959; *The Nine Lives of Island MacKenzie* by Ursula Moray Williams (1980). The theme harks back to Robinson Crusoe and so do the racist biases. Here it is a resourceful lady who is marooned on the desert island, along with a ship's cat, the redoubtable MacKenzie. All proceeds in lively and entertaining fashion, until the arrival one day of a canoe, off which clamber not men or people, but 'savages'. The pictures assist in this demeaning portrayal: tiny ink-black figures with spears twice as tall as they, are shown prancing up the beach. Although Williams needs little help – she puts language to use most skilfully. The 'savages' are never permitted to speak, talk, say or even shout – all they are capable of are 'shrieks', 'yowls', 'yells', 'jabbers' and the occasional 'howl'. As an example of the dehumanizing and degrading of an – albeit imaginary – group of people, this account of their behaviour when they come across that epitome of English civilization, Miss Pettifer's garden, would be hard to beat:

(they) began to shriek and jabber, pointing at it and pulling the flowers – stamping on the flower beds with their wide flat feet. Miss Pettifer ground her teeth with indignation.

When they caught sight of the fire, the effect was electric.

Every savage sprang back and seized his spear or his knobkerry. A deathly silence fell upon them as their heads moved this way and that is if on stalks – seeking danger.

Then, as nothing happened, down on their hands and knees went the whole party, snuffling and pointing at the footprints and pawmarks of Miss Pettifer and MacKenzie which covered the sands . . .

Shofiq – racist or anti-racist?

A novel that has provoked a good deal of debate in relation to race and fiction is *My Mate Shofiq* (1978). Jan Needle, the author, has been heard telling an audience of children's librarians that he wrote it as an anti-racist novel. Certainly, it has been effectively used as one by teachers in secondary classrooms. All the issues are there – the stereotyping, the racial abuse, the prejudices – so as a vehicle for opening up areas for discussion, it can – like so many resources – be made to work.

But the book has been read in other circumstances by children. A school librarian who makes a point of reading new stock and so knew the book, tells how she had *Shofiq* 'slung back at her' by borrowers, who dismissed it as 'a load of rubbish, Miss'. This librarian knew her borrowers as well as her books, so she told them in her view the book was racist – 'at least till near the end' – and the discussion that was opened up in *that* school was illuminating for all concerned.

Many of her readers were black, and their response to *Shofiq* had been to abandon it. The story is told through the eyes of Bernard, a white boy who is quite splendidly realized on the page. He is working class, imaginative, sensitive and street-wise. So realistic does Needle want him to be that he spouts all the current prejudices against Asians – they smell funny, have odd habits, dress strangely, travel on the 'curry train' to the night shift and are, of course, called 'Paki'. And this continues for a good two-thirds of the book. But during these pages, Bernard has become more closely acquainted with one boy, Shofiq, and has come to realize that not only is Shofiq as courageous, enterprising and intelligent as he, Bernard (the hero; the norm) but that he is even beset by the same problem, a mother who is suffering from pathological depression.

So Bernard comes to respect Shofiq and accept him as his friend. What the author has done is to portray a character from an ethnic minority as worthy of the white boy's friendship. Shofiq is given opportunities to prove himself – both to Bernard and to the readers, which he does with flying colours. If one were to apply the role reversal principle here, it is unlikely that Bernard would have had to strive in the same way for acceptance and approval.

Needle has lost some of his black readers along the way, and any white readers who also abandon the book are likely to be left with images in their mind that reinforce 'anti-Paki' graffiti. But even those that persevere with what is a compelling and well-told story may come at the end to view Shofiq simply as a 'good' Paki. They, too, can leave any pejorative stereotype they may have of Asians (which could even have been confirmed by this novel) intact; Shofiq is simply 'different' . . . 'a nice one'. No wonder the Council of

British Pakistanis has taken strong exception to *Shofiq*.

Folktales: a special case?

If we now extend the debate about bias to folktales, and wish to use examples familiar to a British readership looking back to childhood, the references will be mainly European folktales. In which case it is useful to begin with sexist bias and then move to a consideration of racism.

Marion Glastonbury, in her article 'Patriarchal attitudes' (1980) argues cogently against the usual portrayal of women in folktales. The young ones are often merely passive – and very beautiful in, of course, a blonde, blue-eyed way to which Snow White can, by her very name, be permitted to be an exception. They wait for a man, a man who will rescue them from either a desperate situation – Sleeping Beauty, Snow White, Cinderella, Rapunzel – or the desperate prospect of remaining single and thus quite unable to live happily ever after. The older ones are shrewish, greedy, stupid: Glastonbury refers to the tale of the fish and the ring in which the wife of the rewarded fisherman increases her demands 'in a steady crescendo of covetousness from the desire for bread . . . to the final hubris of desiring to rule the world'.

All this relates to the familiar folktales, those of Britain and Northern Europe, which may be frequently parochial – the enemy is in the next kingdom. But among them are many enduring tales that do not confirm attitudes and close the mind. Instead, they allow quite young children to explore profound emotional and moral issues. Stories like *The Three Billy Goats Gruff, Henny-Penny, The Gingerbread Man*, remain deservedly popular among infants. Folktales are a feast, and we can choose what we put upon children's plates.

But, however carefully we select from this European repast, we would still be giving children little more than one view of the world, an eurocentrically biased view. For folktales seek to explain the world – and there are many explanations. If we regard them as all equally valid, then folktales can indeed bridge cultures.

Creation myths of African cultures are now widely available in book form and in English. Some, like the work of Ulli Beier, are translations, others are re-tellings of re-tellings like Barbara Resch's *The Singing Bird* (1977) or that excellent series of myths and legends from many parts of the world published by Oxford. Our children are almost all likely to know *The Tortoise and the Hare*, but how many of them will have learnt that the creator of these immortal competitors, Aesop, was an African?

The oral tradition of many cultures has been tapped for our children. One early spoil of the Raj was Flora Annie Steel's *Tales from the Punjab* (1894). The rich heritage of Indian tales published in India by Thompson Press and Children's Book Trust are now readily available in Britain at bookshops like Soma and Shakti (see organizations listed on p. 160).

Folktales explain why the world is as it is – night and day, earth and water and sky. Or why the sea is salty: according to the *Wise Men of Chelm* (L. Rosten 1982) it is due to all those herrings in it. Children will learn a healthy scepticism from such sages: who also explain the saltiness of herrings was due to their coming out of the sea! Nasreddun, or Hodja can be equally unreliable, but many of his observations about human behaviour offer insights to us all, formed from within the perceptions of a culture very different from the British.

In arguing for continuing to lead children into the world of folktales, I would also like to bring attention to the way that certain concepts and characters become the shared property of two or even several cultures. It seems to happen in two main ways. In many cases, the characters and their stories travel with the storytellers: a classic example is Anansi of Ghana, who is Anansi of the Caribbean (and transmogrified into Brer Rabbit in the Southern States). Anansi the Spiderman (see Share-a-Story, Hallworth, Sherlock, Appaiah) does not always share our British scruples; he has been known to use trickery which could be viewed as stealing – but Anansi is a rebel, a renegade, free of the morals of mortals. This is to be expected. He was the medium through which slaves told stories that defied their masters, and any strategy or trick was perfectly justified. Oddly enough, witches also travelled to the Caribbean, but on boats bound from Europe – Tu Siki is one who took up residence in the West Indies. The British adopted not only the Fox and the Crow from Aesop and Africa, but the Jackal, the Rat and, of course, the Elephant from India, and captured them in books.

More intriguing is the other way in which common concepts occur in different countries. Research for a tale in *Explore-a-Story* (1979) brought to light a striking instance. The concept that if one knows a person's name, it gives power over that person, occurs in at least three separate cultures: in the Viking (and it is this tale that is used in *Explore-a-Story*: 'Reynolds Church'), which itself travelled as 'Tom Tit-Tot:' to Cornwall, as 'Rumpelstilskin' into Germany and occurs more recently in Leguin's *Wizard of Earthsea*; in one group of the American Plain Indians, and again among the San of the Kalahari – where children have a 'given' name, and also a 'true' name known only to themselves and their mother.

To dismiss all folktales then, on the grounds of their sexism – as I heard suggested at a workshop on bias in books – or on the grounds of their reflections of other bias would, I suggest, be to deprive our children of a heritage richer even than that of English literature – it is, after all, the heritage of all the cultures of the world. One can challenge and countermand the sexism, using books like Alison Lurie's: *Clever Gretchen and other forgotten folktales* (1980) and Jay Williams' *The Practical Princess and other liberating fairy tales* (1979).

It is advisable also to be sure that the tale really *is* a folktale, and who the 'folk' is that tells it. In considering books on religion in Chapter 6, I describe one tale in a book of stories for assembly. The 'source' cited is 'Uncle Remus', himself a fictional Southern slave; the tale hinges on the unquestioned assumption that all humans would wish to be white, including the purported storyteller.

Care will inevitably be needed also in selecting what version is used – these books are, after all, retellings for English children, so that writer, editor and illustrator are likely to have an outlook quite different from that of the originator. There is, for example, a retelling that came initially from France of *Beauty and the Beast* (1976) in which the Beast is a golden, hairy, lion-like creature. But when Ladybird published their version in 1976, the beast became not only rather black, but decidedly apelike – a common racist stereotype which occurs also in materials considered in the next chapter. Whether objections to these illustrations came from within the publishing house or from without can only be guessed, but a new illustrator was brought in and a new version published in 1977. All it manages to do is to render the Beast a little greyer, a little less Simian, a little more benign. The model on which 'Beast' is based remains the identical racist stereotype.

The British artist who illustrated Claire Bishop's retelling of *The Five Chinese Brothers* in 1936, has also produced a racist stereotype of a most pernicious kind. The story depends on the idea that the five brothers, each with a magical capacity, look alike, but in the hands of this illustrator, *all* Chinese people look alike. This not only undermines the enchanting tale, it also puts into children's minds images of *how* all Chinese look: yellow, pig-tailed and slant-eyed; identically dressed in two pieces and hats for which there is a special pejorative name. If all this seems 'over-sensitive', consider the reaction of Mr Chan, an Education Officer in Hong Kong who spent time in the U.K. evaluating our education system. He was present when this book was used at a workshop for teachers running the libraries in primary schools. His first reaction was delight at recognizing the familiar when so far from home (something that children do equally joyfully) and perhaps some pleasure that the authority that the U.K. represents still, saw the tale as worthy to incorporate in their institution. But as he leafed through the illustrations, his expression turned to crestfallen distaste. His comment: 'Why don't they do this book again?' Why indeed?

Conclusion

Issues surrounding fiction inform this entire book. Affective learning is the kind that sticks: the information, views and values acquired in the process become part of the unique amalgam of the individual. Much of the general argument pertaining to bias in books is directly applicable to novels and stories, and the *Criteria* reproduced in Chapter 2 devotes a whole section to fiction.

The present chapter extracted fiction, not from the overall concerns of this book, but from the context of books in institutions, i.e. libraries and schools. The next section considers areas of the school curriculum; this chapter addressed the stories read in schools, the novels studied in class, the leisure reading available on loan. For many children in this television and technology age, this will be the only context in which they ever do read fiction. It would be wrong to assume, however, that the imaginative literature thus encountered will not have much impact. There can't be anyone in my readership who hasn't at some time heard, or said, something like: 'I read this book about . . . and afterwards I was never the same/saw things differently/realized that . . .'

But in our rich inheritance of literature for children is the pollutant of racism. The first stories written especially for children were written when Britain was at the height of her imperial power. Today's authors were reared on such books, so that many modern writers simply perpetuate attitudes of anglo-centric white superiority. In remedial and easy readers, the prejudice is exposed and blatant. More enduring fiction is either likely to be more subtle, or may indeed be constructively challenging outmoded attitudes. But 'old' does not equate with 'bad', nor 'new' with 'good'; there is a place for the oldest stories in the world, myths and folktales, although these, too, will need to be selected with care.

Chapter 5

Issues in World Studies

They forgot to ask my name
And called me Negro

Henry Dumas

Bias, particularly racial bias, was identified from the outset as being especially characteristic of children's books on history and geography. Until the 1950s, it was virtually inescapable in any textbook and many of the examples that researchers quote come still from updates of old standbys, such as S. Crawford's *Man Alone* (Longman 1970). Even the title is indicative of the approach: it is true too of many geography and history textbooks that women are invisible. They have little place in recorded history unless they were the rare figures of power. Geography textbooks tend to feature two or three men to every one woman in their photographs of the people of the country. And yet, as the United Nations *Report* of 1980 stated: 'Women constitute half the world's population, perform nearly two thirds of its work hours, receive one fourth of the world's income, and own less than one hundredth of the world's property.'

Sexist bias in history and geography books is really a separate study, and a non-male-oriented, non-hierarchical model for non-sexist and anti-sexist materials needs to be developed alongside the non-racist model illustrated in Diagram 4 at the end of this Chapter. Readers are referred to a model of this approach by Carol Adams (1982) *Ordinary lives: a hundred years ago* (Virago), and to the excellent feminist studies available, particularly: Adams, C. and Laurikietis, R. (1976) *The gender trap: a closer look at sex roles; Book 3 Messages and Images* (Quartet); and Spender, Dale (1982) *Women of Ideas (and what men have done to them)* (Routledge & Kegan Paul).

Rosemary Stones (1983) identifies specific questions we may ask about the way that women (and men) are presented in history such as: Are historical events and developments presented primarily in terms of male activity and achievement?

Stones, R. (1983) *Pour out the cocoa Janet: sexism in children's books.* Longmans Resource Unit for Schools Council (pp21–2).

Returning to the issue of racist bias in relation to the representation in learning resources of people in different places and times, we return briefly to *Man alone.* Seven years ago the publishers, Longmans, began to receive protests about one particular exercise in the book. Pupils are required to list the 'laziest' peoples and the most industrious: the 'laziest' on black paper and their opposites on white. The complaints still come in, but nothing has been changed.

Newer materials have been evaluated by researchers, often in considerable detail. To do justice to this body of work is impossible – all this chapter can attempt is a summary. Readers are referred to the following sources:

Hicks, David W. (1980) *Images of the World*
Hicks, David W. (1981) *Bias in geography textbooks*
Hicks, David W. (1981) *Minorities: a teacher's resource book for the multi-ethnic curriculum*, Heinemann.
Gill, Dawn. 'Assessment in a multicultural society: geography,' summarized in *Multicultural Teaching* vol. 1 no. 2 1982.
African History, what do we teach? London NAME 1978.
Davies, Ann Marie, Hedge, Ann: 'African History in British Schools: a reassessment of the texts in current use,' NAME journal 7 March 1979.
Wright, David: 'A Priority for the Eighties' in *Times Educational Supplement*, 1 April 1983.
Wright, David (1983) 'They have no need of Transport' in *Contemporary Issues in Geography Education* vol. 1 no. 1.

Roy Preiswerk (1980) has provided an analytical grid on 'Forms of ethnocentric distortion', in which he 'identifies':

1 'The ambiguity of the concepts of culture, civilisation and race'
2 'Linear evolutionism' – that other peoples need to 'catch up' to us
3 'Contacts with us are the foundation of their historicity' i.e. the arrogant idea that continents were 'discovered' by the likes of Vasco da Gama or Columbus, when people had been living there for thousands of years
4 'Glorified self-presentation': the European way of life – law,

monotheism, democracy etc. as being the highest stage of
evolution
5   'Unilaterial legitimation of European action' – books that argue
    that the countries exploited by colonialism and slavery actually
    benefitted from the actions of the expansionists
6   'Intercultural and intertemporal transfers of concepts' –
    Preiswerk exemplifies the distortion caused by such transfer in
    the phrase 'They still live in the Stone Age'.

Preiswerk also offers a useful distinction between ethnocentricism and racism: 'The ethnocentric says: our religion is the only true
one, our language is more refined, our material objects are more
sophisticated, our artefacts are more beautiful, we have better
clothes, food, literature and theatre. The racist says: this is only
possible because we are hereditarily superior.' This distinction
allows for the reality that all groups will regard their own group as
central and best – the Europeans are not alone in this. It is the step
farther, the step into racism, that is so rampant in the books that
teach children about the world. Take an example from the *Oxford
Junior Book on Africa*, published in 1969, reprinted until 1974. 'The
Europeans did much good in Africa. They abolished slavery and
stopped the endless fighting between tribes.' There is more than
distortion here – there are half-truths and lies. Nowhere does the
book mention who began slavery; and the 'tribes' (like religious
groups in Europe) are not yet at peace, nor did the Europeans in
any way contribute to any agreement. When guidelines and criteria
for evaluating children's books in terms of bias were drawn up, they
had books like this in mind. *Assessing children's books for a
Multi-ethnic Society* (1980) pleads that 'facts must be accurate'; so
do the criteria for review put out by Leicestershire Libraries, among
many others.

The same paragraph continues:

'They built roads and railways and, later, airports. They set up
schools and hospitals and they built modern towns and improved
agriculture. In fact, they brought Africa in touch with the
modern world. The Africans liked these things . . .'

Here is Preiswerk's number 5 in action, liberally sprinkled with
the attitudes of number 4.
Africa has not been on Oxford's lists for some years now, but is in
use in school libraries all over Britain. It is easy to see why. The
book has a large, attractive format, with a mix of text and coloured
pictures that will tempt pupils to copy their 'project' on Africa from

its pages. The racism is not confined to this one paragraph: it underlies the approach of the whole book, leaving its readers with a view of a continent of people at a lesser stage of development, in which any form of 'civilisation' has existed only since the Europeans brought it, yet where people still practice quaint and exotic customs. So is another generation of schoolchildren misinformed.

This concept of 'civilisation' as existing nowhere in Africa except Ancient Egypt, is one of our enduring racist myths. In 1979. Basil Davidson, attempted to challenge it for children. He had already, in the 1960s and 1970s, effectively disproved it in such words as *Black mother* (1966) and *African Kingdom* (1968). He drew on new technologies of carbon-dating that verify archeological research, and demonstrated conclusively the existence of viable and creative civilizations all over Africa – civilizations that produced not only the bronzes of Benin, the carvings of Ife or the gold weights of the Ashanti, but civilizations that provided a stable society for their members, coping with a challenging and often hostile environment. He helped readers to see them in their own and not in European terms: terms which were recognizably beneficial to their members, offering a worthwhile position for the aged in society, sharing responsibility for the well-being of children. These books may have had a desirable effect on the perceptions of those who read them – presumably other scholars and historians. But Davidson found resistance when he tried to communicate these same facts to children in a book he called *Discovering Africa's Past*. The matter went to the House of Lords, where Lord Brockway strongly defended the book, and Longman duly published it in 1979. The objection to it had been that it was biased!

'Barbarian Blacks' and 'Civilized Whites'

Basil Davidson is a don with a commitment to historical accuracy and as such has made a significant contribution to correcting some of the misapprehensions about Africa that generations of children have gleaned from their textbooks. In an article in the NAME Journal (1978), he quotes (but discreetly does not identify) his predecessor of over fifty years ago as attributing to Africans a 'blank and brutal barbarism' – an enduring and characteristic form of racism that is rife in textbooks. Davidson refutes also the notion of Toynbee that 'civilisation' in Africa began only with the arrival of the white man – but so many and influential are Toynbee's disciples that in textbooks 'black' is equated with 'backward', and the vocabulary does much to reinforce this view. The 'natives' live in 'huts' rather than homes or houses and wear 'costumes' rather than clothing, 'face paint' rather than cosmetics'. They are led not by rulers or kings but by 'chiefs' and defended not by soldiers but by 'warriors'.

Even the appearance of Africans is portrayed in pejorative terms: Townsend, in *Let's visit Kenya, Uganda and Tanzania*, which he *revised* for Burke in 1980 asks 'who are the East African people?' and then describes them thus: 'The earliest immigrants were almost certainly fuzzy-haired, thick-lipped Negroes. Then came the Bantus who were farmers and cattlemen. Although generally lighter-skinned than the pure Negroes, they too had fuzzy hair, flat noses and thick lips.' Already we see an 'improvement', but better still were the next 'tribe' to arrive – the Masai – for they 'originated from Indo-European inhabitants of the Middle East who had mixed with the fierce warrior tribes of Ethiopia'. Small wonder that they are not merely better-armed than any of the earlier arrivals, but also – an amazing assertion – 'quicker-witted'.

Language books themselves accept and promote this Eurocentric arrogance. Jenny Thewlis, in 'Worlds Apart' 1980 cites A. McIver's 1978 reprint of *First Aid in English* as having to pair people and their dwellings thus:

Eskimo – igloo
black fellow – humpy
Red Indian – tepee

As well as being domestically inaccurate in all cases, so that the three right-hand column words have little validity for vocabulary value, there is nothing to be said in favour of the patronizing tone of 'black fellow'. As for 'Eskimo' and 'Red Indian' – both of these terms have been totally rejected by those to whom they have been applied – by whites. Yet the voices of Innuit and American Indians, like those of other peoples, fall often on the deaf ears of the dominant. Only three years ago, I was accused of 'sanitizing' when I criticized a novel, *The Sound of the Gora* (1980) for calling the San characters 'Bushmen' – a term I knew to be a translation of the Afrikaans 'boesman' ascribed by these white invaders to the people they encountered in the bush. The incensed author, Ann Harris, obviously could not resist the pun – unfortunately she also missed the point, which is that it is long overdue that Europeans learn to call groups of people by the name they call themselves.

Shedding the light

Small wonder that 'darkest Africa', described in these terms, had to be 'discovered'. The way in which the Europeans judged and described the lands and peoples they visited was at best paternalistic, more often pejorative. If they are not backward children, they are vicious savages – in 1971 the *Illustrated London News* featured the ruins of Zimbabwe without once acknowledging the fact that these impressive buildings had been built by Africans.

Sivanandan (1982) is one of many who identify this attitude as having been not only intentional, but necessary. How else could colonialism have been justified except as being of benefit to those colonized? And as the 'natives' clearly were the only losers – losers of land and wealth (not to mention power and dignity) – they had to be shown as gaining 'enlightenment'.

The divine right of Empire is epitomized by this quotation from R. Woodcock (1982): 'In the 19th century . . . many European countries began to extend their interests in Africa, dividing the countries south of the Sahara between them. The countries ruled by European powers were called colonies . . .' The picture was one of many cardboard pieces on an Africa-shaped frame, there for the grasping. If there was any protest by the people actually living on those pieces, it was inconvenient and had to be dealt with: 'Africans in canoes attacked Stanley when he was exploring Lake Victoria. Stanley returned later with soldiers to take revenge on his attackers.' (*Explorers* 1981).

Yes, we taught those Africans a lesson! After all, as the first paragraph I quoted continues: 'Now most of Africa is independent, although the new nations have many problems to overcome with widespread poverty and lack of education among their people.' Why this should be so is clearly implied: the Africans are not reeling from a century of exploitation; they are simply backward. This racist attitude is examined later in this chapter.

Explorers are the white heroes of the textbooks; this is general, and also very strongly impressed. A series published by Kestrel with beautiful illustrations in 1979–81, perpetuates these views for to-day's pupils, starting with the 'mysterious continent' image, and the foolish or exotic 'primitiveness' of the people: 'each tribe had a chief, one of (whose) odder tasks was to make it rain – very difficult in dry areas'. (We in Europe are, of course, more successful when we pray for rain!)

The character of Livingstone is distorted ridiculously by the paternalistic perspective: 'Livingstone understood the Africans, while other explorers never tried to. He did not dismiss them just because they were not like Europeans' but then, again, he 'never had any trouble with Africans because they always did just what he said. If he wanted them to stop, they stopped . . .'

A virtual catalogue of this approach can be found in the MacDonald Education version of *Explorers* (1973), which informs – or misinforms – readers, to give only one quote, that Rene Caille was 'the first man to see Timbuktu'.

Newer anthologies of exploration are a little more cautious in their assertions – what has not changed is the explorers themselves, still white, still predominantly European and, except for a few token intrepid long-skirted ladies, still male.

Who matters?

Who and what history is about has largely been determined by the judgment of those who record it. Though historians work from contemporary records, where they are available, the selection they make from those records is designed to accord with what they consider worthy of immortality. A much-quoted but excellent example is that of the nurses of the Crimea: Florence Nightingale is often the token woman in any 'great lives' of the nineteenth century, but Mary Seacole, honoured for her contributions in her lifetime, has been totally disregarded, and this despite the fact that she published a lively and detailed account of her work, available to any historian combing the archives of the era. It has taken two other black women, Ziggy Alexander and Audrey Dewjee, to retrieve that diary, and edit it for Heinemann to publish in 1984. Similarly, archives have recorded a substantial black presence in Britain since the seventeenth century – and substantial evidence of concomitant racism. But not until Walvin and Shyllon each traced and gathered together these documents was any attention paid to this reality: 150 years ago, 4 per cent of London's population was black. These publications were ignored by new writers of textbooks about Britain, so that pupils of the 1970s, unless they were actually exposed to these scholarly books, continued to learn English history that was exclusively white except for the presence of slaves. In 1980, File and Power made the facts accessible to school children at last – but only if teachers and librarians actually use that one particular book: *Black Settlers in Britain 1555–1958*.

Countries in the Caribbean or the South East Asian and South Asian ex-Empire, are retrieving their history from their archives and rewriting their textbooks. Augier and Gordon (1962), for example, have provided a resource from which new textbooks can be prepared for children on the history of the West Indies.

The last two illustrations of how history is distorted have been drawn from A.M. Davies and A. Hedge, who examined *African History in British Schools* (1979). Bibliographical details of the books they quote are indicated (a) to (i) and listed at the end of the chapter.

Slavery

Slavery was a topic much studied when Black Studies were in vogue, and there is a good deal of published material available. Davies and Hedge do not go into the systematic link between slavery and racism – for that we can turn to many sources, among them *Roots of Racism* and *Patterns of Racism* (1982) but they do cite examples from textbooks of the 1960s and 1970s: 'Many of the slaves were criminals or prisoners from the numerous tribal wars. The chieftains would probably have cut their throats if they had not been able to trade them'.[1] However, we can be reassured that 'many slaves were treated still better than domestic pets'.[2]

This dehumanizing of slaves is compounded by what Davies and Hedge condemn as the 'scandalous neglect' of the attitude of black people to slavery, and their role in its abolition, again quoting Cootes: ' . . . before the anti-slavery movement of the late 18th century . . . remarkably few voices were raised in protest against the slave traffic.'

So children learn history without ever hearing of Harriet Tubman, Paul Bogle, Toussaint L'Ouverture, let alone the Maroons who were responsible for over 250 rebellions, making slavery far less financially attractive for the British. They learn only of William Wilberforce, a 'saint' – who himself described the recipients of his single-handed philanthropy of abolition thus:

> the negroes are creatures like ourselves, (but) their minds are
> unformed and their moral characters are debased. In general
> their state of civilisation is very imperfect, their notions of
> morality extremely rude and the powers of their governments
> ill-defined.'[3]

Davies and Hedge conclude that it is not surprising 'that many black pupils in Britain have rejected the whole of their history' and suggest that slavery and how it is presented in textbooks is a key factor in that rejection. 'All children, but at the moment especially black children, deserve to know about the heroic struggle of many slaves to obtain their freedom, through protest, disobedience, and any other means of resistance at their disposal.'

Liberation struggles

Liberation struggles are reviewed by the same authors, in relation to Kenya, (and also Zimbabwe). They point out that few textbooks pay any attention to the 'decades of resistance and sacrifice by the Kenyan people . . . nor the racist, repressive regime under which the black people lived'.

Textbooks instead, presented the uprisings as the sudden eruption of 'a savage and fanatical tribal society'[4] or 'the sadistic and primitive Mau Mau'[5]. It was 'a period of terrible violence mingled with the most primitave witchcraft'[6] and was explained thus: 'the land hunger of the largest tribe, the Kikuyu, led to the eruption of the savage Mau Mau rebellion'[7].

Much was made by textbooks of the tribal rites and 'fanatical' oaths taken by the Africans, where 'animals were sacrificed and the initiates drank their blood and ate their viscera'[8]. But Davies and Hedge found only one textbook that referred to the Hola camp, where British troops detained and tortured Africans, beating eleven to death.

Finally, they observe the textbooks' 'silence on numbers' . . . which creates an impression that many white people were killed in the revolt. Whereas, according to Were and Wilson, 'Ten thousand Mau Mau, two thousand innocent Kikuyu, one thousand Government troops and 58 European and Asian civilians perished'[9].

In the same way, the rebellion in India is taught by the textbooks as a 'Mutiny'. This is so uniform that it is needless to cite titles. The only way to read historical accounts by the English of the Raj is to ask:

Whose interests do the accounts serve?

Clearly it is also not in the interests of the colonizers to mention the immense wealth of India at the time that the British moved in. So very few textbooks do, for then they would have to tackle the question of where that wealth went.

Whether the result of deliberate intent or careless indifference,

65

textbooks that are not written in a way that reflects the interests of those about whom they are written will inevitably be racist. Hum Gar Chan reviewed *The Ancient Chinese* by Lai Po Kan (who is also Katharine Whittaker) and is incensed by the inaccuracies and distortions, such as that the Tang re-unified China, when in reality it was the earlier Sui dynasty, or that in the Han and Tang dynasties 'nearly every family, however poor, had servants who had either been hired or bought'. Equally misleading are the omissions, on which the reviewer comments:

> In a book that claims to inform the reader of 'the everyday life of ordinary people' there is no mention of slavery, peasant rebellions or serfdom . . . nor of secret societies, money-lenders, gay culture or footbinding. The China depicted here engaged in no imperialist wars and was uninfluenced by its northern or western barbarian tribes.

The carelessness is compounded by the illustrations; pictures of Chinese calligraphy give an appearance of authenticity – except that in four cases, these are merely 'meaningless scribble' and in another, the real script is printed upside down.

Indifference allows for the flourishing of ignorance. One instance of this is illustrated by Michael Zeiris (1975):

> It is not specially in the interests of the Europeans to understand that the ability of Aborigines (or American Indians) to track is the result of exact scientific knowledge, knowledge acquired not through 'instructive' but through 'perceptive' education. So 'walkabout' sounds to readers like a mere meander, a directionless post-prandial promenade. Whereas in reality, 'walkabout' describes what are actually clan group movements, made to a preconceived and communicated plan.

The very process of historical research, by delving into earlier writings – and even contemporary documents – written by the dominant group, ensures that unless they consciously challenge the assumptions contained in their sources, the new generation of historians will continue to distort the past in the same racist ways. And indeed, when Davies and Hedges examined newly published history textbooks in 1984, they report finding little change in many areas.

Geography

That similiar questions – who matters, in whose interests is this information selected for inclusion – are pertinent to geography books can be neatly illustrated by an examination of books about South Africa. David Wright, (1983), made a study which found that most geography textbooks use as their picture source none other than the South African Embassy. Publishers find irresistible all this free artwork, no doubt. The result is that whatever the accompanying text, the view that South Africa spends millions of Rand promoting will be reinforced by the impact of the visual images.

Deviance from the norm

Eurocentrism in geography textbooks frequently spills over into racism; any people with a lifestyle different from what the authors consider the British 'norm' must necessarily be inferior. This judgemental aspect goes right through the issues examined in this chapter; here I am looking at the benignly-meant, superficial evaluations, which can nonetheless be offensive.

It is exemplified by the *MacDonald Countries* series, some of which carry their eurocentricism to a point where children could possibly be made to recognize at once the absurd inaccuracies. In *Spain* for example, we are told that 'all Spanish families are alike'. *Italy* describes how men are greatly concerned with their appearance, spending much time at hairdressers and much money on clothes and cosmetics. *India* has had expunged only from its most recent edition, the ludicrous lines: 'Indians have an extraordinary ability for living on top of each other', for which no further explanation is offered. And in *Turkey* we are told, you will soon learn the word for no – yok – which is said with an 'irritating upward jerk of the head'. If in Britain we denote the negative by shaking our heads from side to side, then of course, in terms of the attitude which informs this series, an upward jerk will be 'irritating'. So irritating, in fact, that there is even a caricature of a man making this gesture, complete with 'Yok' in the bubble that comes from his mouth. The same artist may be responsible for the drawing of the representatives of the main castes in *India*, which has given considerable offence to Asians in Britain. The cartoons in MacDonald's *Nigeria* are also demeaning in the way they depict black people.

Simplification, as we have seen, often exposes attitudes particularly nakedly. So it is with the *MacDonald Starters*. They can be examined first in terms of omission: what their creators chose to put in and what to leave out tells us more about anglocentric attitudes than it does about the countries described. Very young children will be sadly misled by the *Starter* on *Kenya* for example, in which the few facts selected for presentation, and the confused arrangement, left one class with the impression that all Kenyans dance – war dances in villages and at discos in towns – that only whites are permitted to shoot lions and that the people resemble apes.

The *Starter* on *Indians* exemplifies how language reflects the attitude of the author and insidiously shapes that of the reader. One page asks: 'How many men are in the picture?' and then: 'who is coming over the hill?' The answer to the second is 'Indians', and clearly they are not part of the answer to the first question. Indians do not, in this text, count as men. The same book reinforces a racist stereotype, that of the naked savage. In a page devoted to pictures of Indians, the largest figure shows a 'Chief' in full head-dress and regalia. There are six other Indians, decreasing in size and as they get smaller, so do their items of clothing decrease and their skins darken, culminating in a miniature bare black 'savage'.

Maps and statistics

That there are 'lies, damn lies and statistics' is such an old saw that its source is lost in time. But the capacity for statistics to bend to the service of any able manipulator can hardly be overestimated. The 'numbers game' is played in all kinds of ways by the media; few of them in the U.K. work to the advantage of ethnic minorities or to people in other countries. Most of us remember the T.V. images of football pitches full of Asians or West Indians so fashionable in the 1960s and 1970s: somehow Oxbridge graduates or Nobel Prize-winners were never counted out against the rest of the population in this way. I am concerned with these images because they are so visually dramatic – long after the actual figures are forgotten, the impact of 'so many of them' lingers in the mind.

Population numbers are often hammered home in much the same way. It would be naive to pretend that there are not many areas which cannot feed their fast-growing populations, yet little account is taken of the family planning drives in South and South East Asia and the particular stringent population growth restrictions in China. And as these are not only the most populous countries but also the poorest and as the eurocentric position is often one of blaming the victim, the idea of too many people = not enough food is fairly embedded in our minds. But there *is*, as Brandt among others has illustrated, enough food to go round – if it were equally shared.

Instead of which, 30 per cent of the world's people (in North America and Europe) consume 80 per cent of the world's food.

Poverty and 'underdevelopment'

A characteristic form of racism has to do with the presentation of poverty in the Third World. Books that gloss over it or deny its existence are misleading; poverty does need to be acknowledged, but it needs also to be explained. Racist books offer a very simple explanation indeed: the people do not work: they are lazy. This judgment passed by racist authors has even been validated in terms of climate:

> The vigorous climate of the temperate regions has encouraged great activity by the white races who occupy them. This can lead to their rapid development. On the other hand, the heat of the tropical areas has tended to make the black races less energetic.
> As a result their progress has been much slower. (Davies, 1970)

Where no explicit reasons for poverty are given, it will be inevitable that the book will implicitly blame the victims. *Living in Calcutta* (1980) has a chapter entitled: 'Poverty and Squalor' which cites heartrending instances, but never suggests the causes: the people simply *are* that way. We do find a clue further on, when we are told 'having friends is considered much more important than having time to clean the kitchen floor'. The step from valuing hospitality above cleanliness (which is merely the author's biased interpretation) is that dirt and squalor are acceptable to Indians.

Geography books that deal more fully with poverty, also often do not locate the causes in colonial exploitation and inequities in trade. Hicks (1981) in *Bias in Georgraphy textbooks* outlines seven points for evaluating how responsibly geography textbooks tackle what, he argues, should be a fundamental question: namely:

'Why are poor countries poor?' It is not, however, a question that many even attempt to answer although they will happily *describe* "third world" poverty.' Out of twenty standard geography books examined by Hicks,

> about a third fail to discuss underdevelopment in any way whatsoever (e.g. Beddis, Young and Lowry); this may in some cases be because that book is thematic or takes a regional approach, although that is not a sufficient reason in itself. A further third only touch on underdevelopment in a vague sort of way. One gains the impression that poverty is something that

just happens to be there (Fawcett), or it is to do with chance (Rice), or somehow to do with a lack of knowledge or inability on the part of the inhabitants (Davies).

Of the remaining six books, two suggest that overpopulation is an important cause of underdevelopment (Long and Robertson, Young and Lowry) whilst the others pay attention to a variety of factors. Rolfe *et al.* offer various indices for measuring development/underdevelopment such as income per head, energy consumption, literacy, occupational structure etc. all of which clearly mark out the 'third world'.

Similarly, Ferris and Toyne list 'obstacles to progress', which it may be worth quoting here. They are: a) poor soils, b) poor cultivation, c) lack of fertiliser, d) poor seeds, e) pests and diseases, f) rainfall, g) religious and social conventions, h) overpopulation, i) transport, j) crop specialisation, k) lack of power, l) lack of experienced workers, m) lack of money, n) waste of money, o) underuse of facilities, p) fear of foreign investors, q) lack of confidence by investors in governments. None of these of course *explain* reasons for 'third world' poverty. In fact almost all of these 'obstacles' prompt the question 'why?' They are in fact some of the *symptoms* of underdevelopment and this is a heading Reed uses when he lists: a) dependence upon agriculture, b) export of primary produce, c) few industries and little power, d) poverty, e) hunger and disease, f) the curtain of ignorance, g) exploding populations, h) where disasters hurt most, i) dependence upon the development countries. Each of these symptoms in fact requires an explanation as to its various interrelated causes.

In conclustion, I offer the following typology.

Typology for racism/anti-racism in books on World Studies

This chapter has dealt with and exemplified the various forms racism can take in textbooks that deal with people in other lands. But though there is more than one form that racism can take, all the examples fit into one model. It is based on a view of the world that has anglocentric western standards at its centre and writ large. As well as being central, this view hovers like a satellite above the world, taking from it those messages that concur with established racist attitudes, scrambling them and further distorting them, and then beaming them out in all their racist bias to the children in the

Diagram 1: Racist perspective

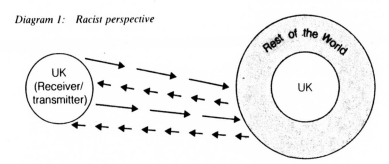

schools. It is possible to illustrate the model in a diagram. The diagram serves also to sum up the chapter thus far.

Attempts have been made to eliminate this racist perspective – to produce what have been termed 'non-racist' books. Authors and publishers have sought to present one area of the world in terms of its own views and values. Generally the focus is very sharp indeed: one child, one family's lifestyle is offered as a case study. This is a practice followed also in some racist writing, but here a conscious effort is made to avoid racist assumptions or judgments in the texts. Examples are A & C Black's BEANS photograph books, also Lutterworth's *How they live now* series. This model would be:

Diagram 2: Non-racist perspective

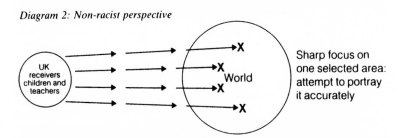

The problem here is in the 'receivers': teachers and children will naturally bring their own value judgments to bear on what they are reading. If their ethnocentricism has developed unchecked, it is easy for them to perceive of themselves as superior: for example Lupita of *Mexico*, who is desperately poor, has to work all day, so does not go to school and get 'educated', or *Sakina in India* whose home is simple in the extreme. 'We don't have a radio or television' she states, which to British children may seem tragic.

Some of the BEANS have elements in them of Diagram 1,

helping to confirm the 'superiority' of western readers. To come back to Juleta of *Zambia*, who does not wear shoes to school, imagine if one of *her* textbooks informed her: 'In Great Britain it is cold and rains often, so John and Jane wear shoes all day long.' And there is another passage in *Zambia* which is perilously close to the 'white man's burden' aspect of racism: 'One day a white man came to visit them. He had come to show them other ways of farming the land so that they could produce more maize.'

Their STRANDS began to be published in 1977 and have been extremely popular. Children have responded positively to having their own identity confirmed, and teachers have welcomed resources that illustrate for all children some of the ethnic minorities now living in the U.K. and the way they live. Hamish Hamilton developed a similar series which, created initially by Joan Solomon, moved from simple narrative to discriptions of religious customs and lifestyles. Commendably, the portrayals of each individual are not only sensitive but painstakingly accurate – as far as they go – though none of the children in the books seem ever to have encountered racism. But the bias within them seeks to be positive; whether the books are received in that way cannot be guaranteed. The bias may be in the eye of the beholder. Even generalizing from positively biased materials can be misleading. Possibly perceiving these pitfalls, MacMillan and Save the Children decided to move away from the convention of publishing separate books on separate lands. The conception of their series *Patterns of Living* (1982) attempts to reduce ethnocentric bias, treating the world in terms of a series of themes. They have thus constructed a new model.

Diagram 3: Thematic approach

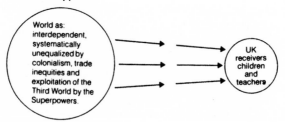

As a model, this appears to reduce ethnocentric and racial bias by putting in perspective for western readers their place in the world. It sets the images of one group of people with several others, impeding the referral back to Europe or the US as the norm. It is no fault of the model that ethnocentric bias *has* crept into some parts of the series, for it has done so simply through omission, such as the presentation of under-development in Lesotho being attributed to only its own lack of industry and poor agricultural prospects. As Hilary Clare (1983) points out, there is no mention that 'until recently, the landlocked little country was a British Colony and that it has been and continues to be at the mercy of South Africa . . . a political satellite and source of cheap labour.'

A fourth model has been developed which deliberately aims to influence and determine the perceptions and attitudes of young readers in the U.K. Acknowledging its source, it can be termed the Development Education model.

Diagram 4: Development education approach

Here the UK, or Europe, or the US, are set within the overall picture, though possibly overemphasized.

Early examples of this model were the World Studies Project publications for children by Robin Richardson published by Nelson. Like *Discovering Africa's Past*, 1979 they were the target for accusations of bias. The bias was readily identified because it opposed and challenged the bias of so many books in lists, and the bias in the books which the accusers had themselves studied as children.

A strategy was developed to try to shift the bias of teachers by encouraging them to reassess their own views of the world and how they were teaching children about it. The World Studies Project published a series of books for teachers including *Debate and decision; seeing and perceiving:films in a world of change* (1979) and *Ideas into action: curriculum for a changing world* (1980) – all still available.

Many of the same arguments were developed for a wider audience by David Hicks (1980) in *Minorities*: he devotes a section to racism in children's books and cites examples of the racist treatment of minorities in textbooks and media such as the EP Filmstrip

Everyday Life among the Australian Aborigines (1960) which for him 'epitomizes all that is bad about teaching materials on minority groups'. The latest initiative involving Dave Hicks is the Schools Council *World Studies Project 8–13*, published this year by Oliver and Boyd. Simon Fisher and he have devised a programme for teachers to explore in the classroom topics like the interdependence of languages, the inequities in trade – who gets how much from a bunch of bananas? – ecology and conservation, armaments and the nuclear threat. They start in the classroom with personal feelings and then move outward: conflict, violence, sexism, racism, power and its abuse. The source material and the classroom programmes are certainly informative and useful: what is particularly relevant to the present study is that people and places are looked at according to a specific set of principles. Writers of history and geography books who take on these principles could be expected to produce the much-needed textbooks schools need to combat racist bias in current materials.

Notes of books quoted by Davies & Hedge:

1 Cootes, R.J., (1977) *Britain since 1700*. Longman.
2 Davies, J.L., (1965) *The Slave Trade and its abolition*. Cape.
3 Gratus, J., (1973) *The Great White Lie*. Monthly Review Press.
4 Duffy, M.N., (1974) *The 20th Century*. Basil Blackwell.
5 Longmate, E., (1974) *Britain 1760–1970*. Philip.
6 Latham, N., (1972) *Africa from pre-history to modern times*. Hulton.
7 Richardson, P., (1972) *Britain, Europe and the Modern World*. Hulton.
8 Hollings, J., (1971) *African Nationalism*. Hart Davis.
9 Were, G.S. and Wilson, D.A., (1976) *East Africa through a Thousand Years*. Evans.

Notes of books quoted by Hicks:

Beddis *et al.*, (1968/75) *Africa, Latin America*. Hodder & Stoughton.
Davies, (1970) *Problems around us*. Holmes McDougall.
Fawcett, (1975) *Spotlight on world problems*. MacMillan.
Ferris and Toyne, (1970) *World Problems*. Hulton.
Long and Robertson, (1969/77) *World Problems*. Hodder & Stoughton.
Rice, (1978) *Patterns in geography* 3. Longman.
Rolfe *et al.*, (1975) *Contrasts in development*. Oxford University Press.

Chapter 6

Bias in materials in other areas of the curriculum

The books considered in this chapter are largely those used in the context of the school curriculum. Collectively, they define the parameters of knowledge considered worth transmitting to children. Whatever is not contained in the stock cupboards and the library is open to an interpretation that it is not worth knowing. The hidden curriculum, plus the cumulative effect of the parameters of the overt curriculum, will be explored more fully in the following chapter. This chapter examines some specific areas of the curriculum and the resources used to teach them. There may be a variation in degree, but bias of the kind with which we are here concerned is present in books across the curriculum.

Art

Books teaching the historical development of art, tend to do so along evolutionary lines which may leave students under a misconception that Renoir is superior to Raphael, Gauguin better than Giotto or Cézanne than Cimabue. S. H.W. Janson's *History of Art for young people* (2nd edn 1982) has, in a text 385 pages long, disposed of all art before that of Ancient Egypt by page 18. Not only is it described as 'Primitive Art', but also by an overall heading of 'The Magic Art of Cavemen and Primitive Peoples'. Yet the illustrations of masks and sculptures by these 'primitive peoples' are all examples clearly captioned as from the nineteenth to the twentieth century, or in the case of the 'Eskimo', the early twentieth century. E.H. Gombrich's classic study, *The Story of Art*, in its twelfth edition (1972) takes an identical approach, titling its first chapter: 'Strange Beginnings; prehistoric and primitive peoples'.

In the art compendia, even the language is often misleading in a way that can be racist. The veracity of landscape depiction by Chinese painters is deprecated by Gombrich's eurocentric evaluations. Or so it reads: Chinese artists from whom 'we must not, of course, expect any portraits of real landscapes', learnt their art by a 'strange method of meditation and concentration in which they first acquired skill in "how to paint pine trees", "how to paint rocks", "how to paint clouds" by studying not nature but the work of renowned masters'. We can dwell for a moment on the use of the word 'strange'; we can also compare this passage with one which describes the 'schools of painting' of the fifteenth century as 'the manner in which the masters of a town handed down their skill and experience to the young generation' – the process is quite differently presented to the reader here.

The way that African art is presented in general histories is also worth scrutiny. Most African art has a purpose: masks or sculptures, murals or brass weights, little was created for 'art's sake' as in the east, India and the west. But the textbooks express this reality rather differently: exquisitely wrought headdresses or masks are used for 'rituals', rituals more likely to be described as 'tribal' than as 'religious'. The whole 'savage/witchdoctor' racist stereotype is reconfirmed by such language.

This Darwinist approach to art has potential for racism: if the arts of Africa or China are dealt with at all, they come, because of their place in history, naturally at the beginning of the book. I have yet to find a textbook that juxtaposes the acme of one civilization's creative art, say the calligraphy and stoneware of the Sung Dynasty in China (eleventh and twelfth centuries) with, say, romanesque mosaics. It would offer little illumination to the student in her appreciation of each, but what it might do is to illustrate that art is not just a steady progression from 'primitive' to 'modern' nor that it improves all along the way.

'Primitive' art is often supported with illustrations from relatively recent times – African, of course. The cave paintings of the San in Southern Africa are followed by other 'tribal' examples; those of Lascaux may well be succeeded by the fripperies of Fragonard or the sophisticated calm of Ingres. Europeans are thus shown to have 'advanced', while Africa stands still. The books featuring the arts of Africa alone tend to be rather less misleading.

There are also the omissions. Many art history books begin with Ancient Egypt, move to Greece and Rome, and then up through the Christian era in the west. Those columns much emulated by Palladian architects who created not only most of our European monumental buildings but cities across India, South East Asia and Africa, are presented to students as being Greek, and given classical names to distinguish their capitals. Whereas the columns are *African*; they were first constructed centuries earlier in temples along the Nile. Greek icons also fall by the wayside: as we get closer to modern times, we narrow the focus of the telescope onto Europe, and then to western Europe. Few art books indicate that the temples of Thailand exceed in scale and splendour the cathedrals of St Peter in Rome or St Paul's in London. Or that within these vast monuments there is work of indescribable refinement. Few art textbooks fail to mention Michelangelo's Pieta in St Peter's, but where are the reproductions of the exquisite and anatomically accurate horse and elephant, vibrant in abalone though each no more than four inches high, mosaiced on the feet of the Reclining Buddha, at his Temple, Wat Po, in Bangkok?

Aesthetes and philosophers like Herbert Read and Roger Fry wrote tomes on the question 'what is art?' but many textbooks have no hesitation in defining what is, and what is not, a work of art. And, whether they do so explicitly or implicity, the answer is eurocentric. It debases or rejects any creation, however glorious, that does not fit into their historical, geographic and aesthetic framework.

Music

Music often receives a similar treatment. The music seen as suitable for study, with a few notable exceptions like the Dartington Hall curriculum (see Frances Shepherd (1982)) is western music. Textbooks endorse – or perhaps determine – this approach. The *Encyclopaedia of Music* (1979), for example, describes only those instruments used in European orchestras, and the authoritative P.A. Scholes (1970) *Oxford Companion to Music*, even in his tenth edition, focuses on European music, though it does graciously include jazz!

A 'bandwagon' approach is rife in the compendium-style books on music, by which I mean that some of the publishers became aware that there was a demand for materials that would present a more global view of music, and that jumping on this bandwagon might sell more copies. What they did not trouble to develop was an awareness of how this should be done, and contented themselves with a tokenist gesture, such as the one Indian painting that makes up one-fifth of the collage of musicians and instruments adorning the cover of *The World of Musical Instruments* (1972) which is never mentioned in the text; or a complacent eurocentric judgment, of which this excerpt from the *Oxford Junior Companion to Music* (1979) on the subject of dance is a gem:

'. . . Whether it be in the primitive rituals of a tribe, the stately patterns of an 18th century minuet, the langorous swirl of the 19th century waltz, or the jerkiness of today's popular dances' (described in the preceding paragraph as nearer to the style of 'primitive tribes') 'you get a clear picture of the kind of life and values of the people that danced them.'

If Indian music is taught, then separate resources have to be used. Oxford has published *Indian Musical Instruments* (1978), which could provide a useful starting point. But it means that the study of Indian music is not integrated into the general study of music – the eurocentric textbooks have firmly kept it out. Moreover, to do justice to a separate study would fill the music timetable: the Indian sub-continent has produced more instruments that any other region. Whereas European music, at least till very recently, is based on a beat of four, the rhythms of Indian music are immensely complex and varied, with counts of seven, twelve and even fifteen. Much easier to dismiss it all as merely folk or 'ethnic' music, something exotic, than to try to teach the complexities of the raga. The implications for the timetable of all this are very serious, and will be dealt with in some depth in chapter 7.

Language primers and reading support books

Nor are language books exempt from bias. How languages are rated, and the treatment of community languages, are other issues examined in the next chapter. Here it is language teaching materials that come under scrutiny.

Modern language primers set out to give a view of the relevant country, so that the language learning can be set in context. The new textbooks being developed in Germany for children learning English as a foreign language, are taking care in their illustrations to reflect the racial diversity in British cities. But when I scan, for example, the French primers in use in British schools, even those published in the 1980s portray Paris as an all-white area. No account is taken of the two million West Africans and North Africans who have settled in France, many in the capital city.

Vetting books in other languages is not easy, yet it is likely to be necessary. The National Children's Librarian of Singapore, V.

Perambulavil (1983), has recorded the problem. Careful attention was paid to the racist bias in their collection of children's books in English, and many of the writers of colonial times – the Johns, Loftings and Blytons, have been replaced. But with three other official languages to cater for, Chinese, Malay and Tamil, all with a far less developed written tradition for children and so a heavy reliance on translations from English, her staff have to be vigilant against the same racist stories 'creeping in by the back door'. This can happen anywhere, and is particularly likely in the case of a language with a strong oral tradition but still little development of books for children. Which explains why a Turkish shop in London in the 1970s was selling a little paperback in Turkish of short stories for children, one of which was unmistakeably identifiable from the illustrations as *Little Black Sambo*.

Materials designed to teach English as a Second Language are often developed within schools or ESL centres. They, and the nationally published resources such as *Scope* (1971) are sensitive to their clientele. Any bias that is operating is likely to be positive towards the bilingual users. Fortunately, not many schools today use textbooks to teach English to the English, for these primers were often eurocentric in the extreme.

English as Mother Tongue is now taught through a range of literature and anthologies of snippets from literature, generally selected quite carefully. Longman's series of graded readers, for example, takes care to include writings in English from the Caribbean, Africa and black Americans, and specific anthologies such as *Merrywhang* on Caribbean literature, are also in use.

It is in the remedial reading cupboard that simplistic books that bare racism to its most blatant will be found. *Crow and the Brown Boy* by Joan Tate (1976) is of the *genre* so popular that no large English children's book publisher neglected to bring out at least one series in the 1970s – the 'high-interest age, low reading age' books that cram the remedial stock cupboards in our schools. The story is about Jim, a white boy, who, when he wants to replace a no longer adequate bicycle, takes on a paper round to earn the money for a new one. A boy of this calibre can be expected to do what he can to help the young black crow he encounters one early morning, for even though it is not a lovely bird, it is injured and cannot get about much to find food. Jim, therefore, pockets extra bread, which he brings to the crow each morning. So appreciative is the crow that it becomes tame enough to sit on his shoulder. A banal story, but harmless enough, until an analogous plot develops. One morning Jim finds no crow – and no bread. Investigating, he discovers lurking in the bushes, another boy. The next line stands in separated clarity: 'A brown boy'.

This is followed by a description of the brown boy, which tells us that he has black curly hair and big brown eyes – nothing about his age, size, dress. The story continues:

'His eyes rolled when he saw Jim looking at him.' Her readers do not need to be told that Jim's eyes remain steadfastly fixed, only that 'In his hand was the bread, the bread that Jim had brought for the crow'.

The brown boy implores Jim not to hit him.

There is more to come. The brown boy is a starving West Indian immigrant named Lazarus(!) whom Jim duly raises by making sandwiches each morning, which he wraps and leaves under the bushes. And Lazarus, too, is duly tamed: a picture confirms that: 'Now Jim had two friends for breakfast'.

Tate continues to spell out the analogy for her slow readers right to the end. The next development is that Jim has earned enough to replace that old bike – but it is quite good enough for Lazarus, as a picture of both of them pedalling along illustrates. The crow, too, has made progress, and flies off, prompting Lazarus in the very last lines, to behave thus:

Smile his big white smile and flew off on his *new* bike (italics mine).

Primary schools will find reading support materials that are equally expressive of bias. Sparks, on the whole a carefully conceived series, and one of the earliest to reflect ethnic minority children in a lively and positive way – such as their *Upside Down Vera* (1975) – features a book called *Mumbo Jumbo* (1976). As the title indicates, it is the mystical rites of savage tribes that are conjured up here – luckily the white children who have been drawn into this primitive world by the magic of a mask escape – for there is really no knowing what these savages may have done to them: the worst is only hinted at. For younger readers still, *Here are the Brick Street Boys* (1974), ends with an explicit picture of the caricatured stereotype cannibals complete with bones through their noses, round a pot in which is simmering the hated football referee.

This was one of the earlier efforts at attracting a multicultural market, published in 1974. Publishers and writers identified a new bandwagon, and then jumped on. Predictably, the results were, as in this case, ill-considered, or at best tokenist (the Brick Street Boys themselves include one black boy). Ladybird browned up one Caucasian face on the covers of some of their publications; inside, however, the faces remain uniformly pink.

The Ahlbergs, authors of the Brick Street series, have moved on. One recent character of theirs from an ethnic minority is Mrs Cosmo who 'wears a sari and a tikka . . . never eats a chappati, doesn't go to the Gurdwara . . . balance pigeons in the family magic show and allows Mr Cosmo to decide when the caravan has to leave'. Farrukh Dhondy (1983) is not too impressed with this either, commenting: 'some efforts carry this self-conscious intrusion a bit far'. His central point is most important: works which he describes as 'created by the missions of critical consciousness' are of little value (to which I would add that they may be of some value, but of a short-lived nature) and should not be confused with 'real' literature.

Reading schemes

Once we consider reading schemes themselves, racism and sexism are rife, and they have been widely attacked. Enfield Teachers' Centre has produced a study of racism (1980). Cynthia Knight's (1983) analysis of three recent reading schemes shows that there has been little improvement.

Teachers have also taken strong exception to the *Bangers and Mash* series because of the illustrations of the black family. The publishers, Longmans, argue that all the pictures are cartoons, and that the white families are caricatures also. But it is the *manner* in which the blacks are caricatured that is racist: their lips are grotesquely thickened and their noses spread virtually from ear to ear. Cartoons, like comics, by their very nature emphasize differences; once an element of ridicule is added, the resulting treatment of ethnic minorities is inevitably racist.

Also widely attacked are two of MacMillan's Nippers, *Visitor from Home* (1973) and *New People at 24* (1973). These Nippers are among several written by Beryl Gilroy, herself black and at the time a headteacher. Her argument is persuasive: she wrote these books for black children, and those children would be encountering racism in our society, so should meet it first in the 'safe' context of a book, where it can be more easily handled. All of which cannot be faulted. But I believe that the racism must indeed be handled, and refuted immediately, and *New People at 24* does not do so.

Gilroy has used the Alf Garnett device of putting the racist comments in the mouth of one character, the white grandmother. 'Let's hope foreigners don't get hold of that poor (empty) house. I don't have anything against foreigners, but English people should live in English houses. After all, we don't run to Bongoland to live in their huts.'

Those comments are indeed ridiculed by the two main characters, one white boy and one black (called Roy) for Roy considers this 'a soppy thing to say', and both boys 'shout with laughter'. Then Roy asks 'what's foreigners', and on being told 'people who come from foreign parts, I suppose. People like you. Black people,' replies: 'I don't come from foreign parts, I was born here. But my mum and dad are Bajans from Barbados. They aren't foreigners. My dad drives trains. He's a traindriver. That's what he is, not a foreigner'.

A refutation, of a kind, though possibly not very satisfactory. However, one remark has been allowed to slip by unchallenged: the nonsensical 'Bongoland' where people live in 'huts' conjures up for the readers yet another image to add to the residue of grass-skirted, primitive blacks. And Granny's final acceptance of the couple she has termed as 'black and white minstrels' (another image best left to die) turns again on the 'he's a good one' syndrome that permits the stereotype to remain intact. As Preiswerk (1980) indicates 'there is no evidence in all the research done on human knowledge that an "insider" is by definition better qualified to speak about the group he (sic) belongs to'. Particularly when 'he' is projecting the pejorative bias of the dominant, outside groups. It remains to be said about the 'Nippers' that they are no longer widely used as a reading scheme, but they are sturdy and attractive books, and are made available in many schools as a supplement to the library i.e. for children to take to their homes and read to themselves. Furthermore, whoever Gilroy wrote them for, their readership in the UK will, as with all books, be largely white.

Religious Education and assemblies

Primary assembly books, like the Religious Education resources in secondary schools, can, if not predicated upon a comparative religion stance, be biased against any religion other than Christianity. There are anthologies for assemblies that are based entirely on the assumption that all the children to whom it is addressed are Christians – or should be. Proselityzing is no longer a strong characteristic of mainstream Christian faith, and many church organizations have promoted interfaith understanding and respect. Some of their work is considered in the sections on strategy for the combat of bias, but acknowledgment should be made here of at least the following (listed in full in organizations): AFFOR, Catholic Commission for Racial Justice, World Council of Churches, British Council of Churches as well as the work of Quakers.

Injudicious use of assembly anthologies can have the deplorable effect of actually preaching and teaching racism from the rostrum of the school hall. Consider the story 'Why the Negro is black' (Carr, 1981).

Uncle Remus, the coloured storyteller, was making shoelaces. The little boy who was watching him noticed that the palms of his hands were as white as his own. He asked the reason for this, hoping that the old man would reply with a good story. He was not disappointed.

Far back in the old days, Uncle Remus told him, everyone was black. The English, the Chinese, the Eskimos – all were as dark-skinned as Africans. There were no people of any other colour. Then there came news of a magic pond. It was said that anyone who bathed in its waters would come out white-skinned. Most people laughed at the story. It was just a fairy tale, they scoffed. There was no such pond. One man set out to find it. When he returned to his family they thought their eyes were playing tricks. His skin was as pale as a summer cloud.

All of a sudden everybody wanted to be white! Thousands rushed headlong towards the pond. The quickest runners plunged in first. They emerged as white men, delighted with their newly bleached skin. Others dived in after them, with the same result. Soon the pool was alive with laughing palefaces. Crowds pushed and struggled on its banks, eager to jump in. Before long the level of water had sunk, for everyone used up a little. A short while later it was no deeper than a fish-tank. Latecomers could only scoop up handfuls and splash themselves. They came out with pale yellow skins and went off to live in China.

At last there was no water left. Those who had come last walked barefoot on the wet bed of the pond. They bent down and pressed their palms on the damp earth. Then, still dark-skinned, they set out for their home in Africa. Only the soles of their feet and the palms of their hands were white.

That is why some men are black, Uncle Remus told the little boy. It is a charming story but it is not really true. We now know that colouring matter in the skin gives Negroes their dark complexion. This helps them to withstand the effects of the hot African sun. Inside their skin they are just like everybody else.

That this tale appears to be told by a black man makes the basic theme that to become white is to achieve success even more accepted. In fact, the story is acknowledged as being an adaptation from Joel Chandler Harris, who created the fictional character of

'Uncle Remus', one very reassuring to white readers, last century. But Frank Carr's compilation, as may have been noted, was published in 1981.

The textbooks that teach Religious Education as an examination subject may also give cause for alarm. It is the rule rather than the exception that the books written about the non-Christian religions are not by members of the faith being described. It is rare to find a writer like Richard Tames (1982) (*World of Islam*) or Patricia Bahree (1982) *The Hindu World* who understand both the faith they describe and the likely stance of the majority of their readers. Thame, for example, smashes one stereotype with the very first picture, on page 1: it shows an Arab in a kefiya and has the caption: 'many people think of Muslims as being Arabs. In fact Arabs make up only about one-sixth of the world's Muslim population'.

More common are writers who, however scholarly and thorough their research, view other religions than Christianity, from an outside viewpoint, which usually means a dominant Christian one. However scholarly their approach to what they acknowledge as 'World Religions'; if they are convinced that theirs is the only 'true' religion, it will be inevitable that they will view other religions as 'primitive'. R. Bruce and J. Wallbank (1982) epitomize this form of racism. Page 45 consists of a picture of a white-capped black man crouching before a bamboo screen with one hand on a cobra, surrounded by piles of undefinable planks and other materials. None is recognizably sinister, but the caption invites particular kinds of answers. It reads: 'A witchcraft stall in Africa. What is being sold and what do you think they are being used for?' The picture of the diviner or seer is even more overtly 'primitive' – indeed, the toothy mask, skulls in lap and bones on the ground prompt the reader to thoughts of cannibals. Is it meant to be funny? I think the illustration captioned 'Recipes for Success?' is actually so intended: here our savage is reading from 'Batty Haddocks Book of Potions' and throwing into a pot items from packages with 'humorous' labels such as 'Cockroaches – new crunchy recipe', 'Maggots – economy size' and 'Bats' blood'. All in a book purporting to teach our children, in 1982, about *religion*. But then this same page vindicates the authors from any blasphemy, for they tell their readers: 'There are many strange stories of people dying at the hand of an evil holy man. Many of them sound very much like superstitions.' But so are the practices of most religious groups when reduced to the ridiculous.

Often a religion is portrayed only through some of the customs observed, with no attempt to explore the fundamental principles of the faith. The results inevitably reduce the religion to something quaint, odd and exotic: 'just look at what these Sikhs/Jews/Moslems do.' A relatively new series *Friends and Neighbours* by D.G. Butler (1982), exemplifies this deprecating approach. It is as well to remember that though such books purport to explain the religions of minority groups these are *not* minority religions. Followers of Buddhism, Islam and Hindu are among many that outnumber the followers of Christianity, and they are spread across the globe.

Because of their orientation, many Religious Education textbooks will be found inappropriate if the school adopts a comparative, or ecumenical, approach to its Religious Education curriculum. That is: that all religions are equally recognized as providing for their followers a rationale for living, spiritual support in their daily lives and in time of need such as bereavement, the patterns by which to observe the milestones of pairing, birth, death, and providing also the ethics and the rules that permit them to live peaceably together. The Ten Commandments, the Eight Paths of Righteousness and the Fivefold Path are substantially the same: laws made by religious leaders before it became a matter for secular legislation and jurisdiction.

Another form of bias in Religious Education books relates closely to the ethnocentric and racist attitudes identified in the previous chapter, and to which Roy Preiswerk's grid (see p. 58) may be applied. Doing good to others for no visible gain in this world is a feature of most religions; unfortunately in the context of Christianity it sometimes smacks of paternalism. Partly, it is a legacy of the missionary era, when any 'native' could be described as a 'heathen' and baptism was the only way to save a soul; clothing and converting the only way to 'civilize' and 'improve'. Partly, it is that charity connotes inequality: it is the 'superior' who bestow it upon the 'inferior'. Both Patricia Bidol and David Ruddell (1983) make this point in their race awareness programmes, 'Helping is racist, sharing is equitable'. Alms to the poor go too often from white hands to black: the images on posters of starving children in Asia or Africa for which Christian Aid and Oxfam have been so criticized, are the images of many Religious Education books. As in geography books, the real reasons that these people are starving and would now indeed benefit from help and charity, are never even indicated. This leaves the interpretation by children open to the view that it is 'heathen' who are poor. We, the superior group, are there to help and be kind to them – it is as heroic an action as that of our Crusaders who brought Christianity to people they called 'non-believers'.

While charity, in these terms, is an outdated and racist 'morality' to perpetuate in religious instruction, there is a moral issue we might *expect* to find in modern textbooks for Religious Education: the feelings and behaviour of the dominant group towards ethnic minority groups and individuals that they encounter in school and the community, and the way they regard people of other background or in other countries. If religious instruction is to continue to have a moral dimension, surely a part of it must be to instil a respect for the rights and dignity of minorities? The British Council of Churches has taken this on in their education programme. Their tape slide: *The Enemy Within* is one example, and it is significant that one book much cited here, *The Slant of the Pen*, was developed by the World Council of Churches.

Mathematics

Resources for teaching sciences, mathematics, craft design and technology are almost exclusively ethnocentric. Omission on a large scale can endorse a hidden curriculum that is racist and sexist, that proclaims that only white children – and in most cases only white boys – conduct experiments in physics or chemistry, make mathematical measurements or design and construct. That, in fact, no other children exist, or at least not in circumstances worth acknowledging.

The first movements by educational publishers to adjust this bias was predictably tokenist: Fletcher's *Mathematics* added a scatter of black faces among the white, which was welcomed by campaigners as better than nothing. This was 1976 and it is fair to say that both the publishers and their consumers shared a view that this shift was of value for black children. The perceived market was restricted to inner city schools which were ethnically diverse; on this there was general agreement. So general that publishers' representatives took it as inevitable that the selectors of textbooks for science and technology subjects in the white shires would consciously reject resources with even token black representation on grounds that 'we don't have any of them here'. This attitude is now being challenged by initiatives and training for multicultural education but is proving particularly hard to alter in the sciences. Until there is a shift in this still considerable part of the market, however, there will be white children going through our education system who encounter in their schools only a biased view of the world as either (1) exclusively white, like all the people they see in their community or (2) where it is only white people who learn to master scientific and technological skills. Add to this the confirmation that these skills and studies are presented also as the prerogative of boys only, and the resources have, individually and collectively, beamed a racist and sexist message to all who use them.

Mathematics is presented in textbooks as a western science; pupils learn about Archimedes and Pythagoras, but not about the development of our numerals from the Devangari system developed in India about 1200 years ago. Misled by omission, pupils are more likely to believe that Roman numerals were simply superseded by 'European' numbers, whereas what happened was that Arab traders, as recently as the seventeenth century, became exasperated with calculating in Roman numerals and introduced the Devangari letters into the west. Also from India, they brought the concept of negative numbers, on the other side of zero from the positive. By so doing, the Islamic traders equipped themselves with the technique for pen and paper calculations: the zero and minus numbers represented debts; the development of the base ten to 'borrow' facilitated subtractions. No wonder the west readily adopted these Hindu techniques of calculation, now taught as 'ours'. Alistair Ross's (1984) is the only English textbook to date that attempts to correct the racist inaccuracy about the origins of 'our' mathematics, aimed at primary level. It complements the work of Ray Hemmings (1983 and 1984), which considers number patterns for primary children, as well as more complex mathematical structures through secondary school.

Further help is available from the United States in the work of Claudia Zaslavsky. As well as an illuminating book for teachers: *Africa counts; number and pattern in African culture* (1979), she has produced two very attractive classroom resources. For younger mathematicians, there is *Count on your fingers African style* (1981) which explores some quite sophisticated inter-relationships of numbers in the context of the market women of Africa's totalling of items and cost. *Tic Tac Toe* (1982) celebrates for the middle school a game (the British version would be 'Noughts and crosses') which is played in various forms all over the world, and the principle of which is also that of binary computers.

Textbooks for mathematics have not extended their parameters to take into account these mathematical principles or principles of measurement such as those devised for the calculating of amounts of gold-dust – necessarily very precise indeed – by the Ashanti. However, they do take odd darts beyond Britain's boundaries. Back into the joke world of the racist stereotype, exemplified in

O + B Maths Bank II (Oliver and Boyd, 1979). This is a book of mathematical exercises designed for pupils to work through on their own. Though topical and apparently relevant, the author or publisher must have deemed it necessary to offer intermittent rewards to the student, in the form of little cartoons. And there is the white man in the pot, flanked by eager cannibals. Twice over in fact, as one pot is over an open fire while the other is over a gas cooker. 'Humour' is also provided in the drawing that accompanies the legend 'I open my mouth and tip up my cup', the joke being that the fool so doing is holding the cup over his head, so that the liquid cascades on to it. And the fool is not only black, but a particularly exaggerated caricature, totally gratuitous and extremely offensive. If one pauses to consider what the purpose of such cruel and crude adornments to a straight mathematics text could have been, one is led to suspect that such a cheap 'joke' was *intentionally* racist.

Science

Two particularly blatant forms of racist bias occur in science materials. Let us deal first with *omission* specifically as it relates to science. As with most mathematical texts, black people are simply not seen: that is, they do not conduct experiments in physics or chemistry and, more perniciously they have not contributed to scientific development. Yet iron ore, for instance, was processed in furnaces in Africa long before Europe.

Not only are black women and men invisible in the books about science past and present, but the future, publications suggest, has no place for them either. Look, for example, at *The Future* (Gatland, 1982). This sturdy book is vividly and lavishly illustrated in the style of a magazine and is clearly aimed to appeal to young people and stimulate them to imagine an excitingly different future. But it is clear that in the future here envisaged, women will still have a subservient role and it will be whites who *man* the machines and control the brave new world.

The second issue is more fundamental and pervades much of thinking and thus of learning. So significant is it in any consideration of racism that the rest of this chapter is devoted to the implications of *biological determinism* to our study. It is based largely on a paper given by Professor Steven Rose in June 1984 in a series on the history of racism in the west and, while it is impossible to do justice in a summary, his analysis demonstrates how scientific studies were conducted from a racist perspective and their findings were further used to support racism with a 'scientific' legitimacy.

Rose located the rise of scientific racism in the nineteenth century, not because that was the beginning of racism, but because this was the period in which science triumphed over the church as the interpreter and explainer of the world. So inevitably in a racist society, science would be put to use to legitimate the superiority of the white 'race'. It would provide justification on these new scientific grounds for the colonial exploitation of those lesser beings unable to manage for themselves; justification for a society in which, then and now, the people in power in all walks of life from government through law, medicine, education and industry are practically without exception white.

Rose analyses how the process goes further still. The way in which science developed in the west ensured that racism would be built in as an inevitable feature of that science and of scientific method. He argues that Darwinian evolutionary theory substantiated all racial genetics. The very core of this thinking was based on the power of heredity in tandem with an acceptance of 'the claim of racial superiority by one identifiable race over another' – Rose's very definition of racism. He cites the Couvier 'Scale of Perfectability', which was based on minutely precise 'scientific' measurement of the angle of jaw and brow. Skull sizes were also measured and equated with both intelligence level and racial determinants. There existed also an obsessional 'Index of Negrescence' whereby skin colour was measured with similar 'scientific' precision. This led to the American school of psychology/psychometry of the 1920s and 1930s which led in turn to the eugenics movement, calling for compulsory sterilization of all people with an IQ below a particular figure. In the States, Rose maintains, it was racism that required buttressing by science – in the UK science was put to the same use with regard to class: Francis Galton developed a technique of proving that genius was inherited – especially by white British upper classes – by 'measuring' the achievers.

Rose identifies one further way in which the development of western science, along with trade and social patterns, guaranteed its racist character. It was posited upon the de-development of Africa and Asia and on the de-development of science in those countries, with unfortunate and lasting consequences for scientific study in those countries whose scholars may now rely on western modes of approach. And in the west itself the analytical reductionist mode *must* be racist and sexist. Nor has the west outgrown it: the same claims are being made by psychometrists and geneticists today in defence of the ruling *status quo*. And all this despite the fact that, as

Rose stated initially, 'modern biology has little use for a concept of race; race is a social, not a biological factor.'

This, then, is the bare bones of the thesis that science has been used to legitimize racism; that reductionism ceased to be a progressive force and became used as an oppressive one. When asked where we can begin to instigate change, Rose has a noteworthy answer – we can begin by changing in schools 'the automatic assumptions of the value-neutrality of science.'

In learning the science that they then pass on to pupils, teachers absorb the racist values inherent in the discipline. The materials for children echo the racism – in practically every book that divides humankind into 'Mongoloid, Negroid and Caucasian', it is clear which 'race' is presumed as inherently superior. The myth of the value neutrality of the subject is seldom challenged. It spills over into the applied sciences and technology: the only time black people are likely to be featured is performing agricultural tasks, generally the menial ones, making little use of modern farming technology. The children handling these books, whether they be black or white, will be left in little doubt as to who is the most 'advanced' and 'superior race'. And even will remain so, as our glimpse into books about the future illustrated.

Conclusion

Learning materials have been shown to give biased information. Only certain aspects of the world's art, music and religious practices and beliefs are endorsed as being worthy of detailed study; others are set against them as being less sophisticated, exotic and certainly of less significance. A eurocentric 'Christian' perspective on Religious Instruction may be unhelpful to Christians and offensive to observers of other faiths. We should, however, be aware of the significant initiatives from Christian organizations to adopt a radically different stance, one which supports the validity and power of all religions.

Language primers and reading schemes are likely to present a world in which all of Europe is white and to uphold sex role stereotypes. And high-low readers may approach characters from such a simplistic and stereotypical viewpoint that they portray people from other cultures in the same oversimplified racist manner as do comic books.

Science is taught as being objective, neutral and value-free. Yet because science has developed in the west at a time when racism was entrenched in society, it upholds that racism within the discipline. In order to countermand the 'scientific' validation of the superiority of the white 'race', it is essential to teach children that (a) science as presented in textbooks is *not* value-free, (b) race is *not* a concept that can be validated by the science of biology and (c) the ethnic variation in modern human kind is *not* part of an evolutionary chain with "Europeans" at the top. Unfortunately, science books almost all present precisely the opposite view.

Most authoritative of all, both in the way they are presented and in the way they are viewed by adults and children alike, are encyclopedias: by their tone, their evident scholarship and their sheer volume, they appear to enshrine all the knowledge worth knowing – knowledge, however selected from a eurocentric viewpoint. Furthermore, encyclopedias claim an objective, value-free stance which they do not substantiate: the information is gleaned from 'experts' but there is no acknowledgment that each expert has his or her own values and attitudes. Users of encyclopedias and non-fiction books and learning materials are mistaken if they assume that the information within them is pure, objective 'fact'.

Chapter 7

The cumulative and the concealed: curriculum implications

A class of nine to ten year olds in a Surrey middle school were given a vocabulary exercise, naming the female and offspring associated with words such as:-
Ram? Ewe, lamb; Fox? Vixen, cub; Negro? – to which a pupil replied: 'Negress, child'. 'Child' was struck out, and the teacher substituted 'Picanninny'. Reported in *The Times*, 26 April 1983.

Collectively, the resources in schools often reflect and reconfirm the attitudes of teachers, acquired in *their* schooldays, unless a conscious effort is made to examine and re-evaluate them. Education is, after all, a process of continuity and change; resources are one area where changes are likely to be necessary.

Unless there are changes, the materials can give children an extremely biased view of what it is that they need to know in order to 'get on' in the world. The art worth emulating, the music worth making, the languages worth learning will, in a school that has not seen fit to reappraise its resources, be almost exclusively European. Where the resources do make mention of the existence of, say, music or language of Africa or Asia, they are evaluated from the viewpoint that Preiswerk (1980) describes, as beyond the ethnocentric and into the racist; i.e. that the European contributions are indubitably superior. Indeed the heritage of rich cultures may be not only dismissed but denied: the *History of Europe* by H.A.L. Fisher (1969) states:

> to the conquest of nature through knowledge, the contributions made by Asiatics have been negligible and by Africans (Egyptians excluded) non-existent . . . all the leading discoveries . . . are the result of researches carried out by white men of European stock.

The traditional curriculum of western schools in the UK is still based upon the 'Classics'. Greek and even Latin may have been dropped from the secondary syllabus, but many of the subjects retained – and the perceived parameters of knowledge in each – reflect their origins in a system where education was restricted to the privileged, and designed to perpetuate their privilege.

Physics, chemistry, mathematics, history, geography, European languages, literature and art were, with the addition of astronomy, philosophy, politics and of course the Classics themselves, the areas of knowledge explored by Renaissance man. If anything, the emphasis has become more narrowly academic: discursive studies like philosophy have been all but abandoned and politics is only beginning to make a comeback. With the exception of Computer Science, which is a pragmatic response to technological advance, recently introduced subjects are generally 'soft options' or seen that way by teachers and pupils alike. Craft, design and technology (CDT), pottery and other crafts, home economics and, amazingly, even sociology and economics, are what the less able pupils are encouraged to specialize in. Sport is also assumed to be best done by the less academic pupils, and where the school has an ethos that permits teacher expectations to be lower for their black pupils, it is blacks who are encouraged to the tracks, often at the cost of their examination qualifications. This last phenomenon is far from uncommon in schools in the UK and is discussed by Bruce Carrington and E. Wood in 'Body Talk: Images of Sport in a Multiracial School'. (1983)

The issues are explained fully by a number of sociologists who have noticed that all societies define what constitutes high status knowledge, and how it is evaluated and that the ways in which this is made available to different categories of young people through the curriculum is one of the most important mechanisms of social control. The issues are clearly explained by Eggleston (1977). It is clear that a genuinely racist-free curriculum must not only tackle the presentations of knowledge and understanding but also the fundamental issues of the *distribution* of knowledge, the *evaluation* of knowledge and most fundamentally the *definition* of what counts as knowledge in a society.

School library books endorse even this racist practice: the first biographies of contemporary blacks to be published in the UK were of Martin Luther King and Cassius Clay. Next came Bob Marley and the traditional jazz musicians. For books on Mahatma Gandhi, one had to import publications from the Indian sub-continent – fortunately easily done – and the same procedure was needed for other important religious leaders such as Guru Nanak or the Prophet Mohammed.

The 'biography' section in the school library is likely to suggest that only white people – mostly men – ever did anything of note that merited having books written about them. One does not even need to take them off the shelves to get this message: a reason perhaps why in some schools, few students do. The students are familiar to the point of contempt with Livingstone, Marco Polo and Queen Victoria. They might be more eager to read, and be enlightened by, a biography of Mary Seacole.

She presents a good example, in fact, of who matters in the view of society – as reflected by authors, publishers and purchasers of their products – and of individual schools. Mary Seacole travelled from her home in Jamaica to the Crimea and she, like Nightingale, nursed British soldiers in conditions which she radically improved. She set up her own convalescent home for soldiers, saving so many lives that the British Government decorated her for her contribution even though they had rejected her as a nurse because of her colour. Nevertheless, she was allowed to become destitute after the war ended. Her story was recorded for children only in N. File and C. Power (1980) and in *Roots in Britain*, an exhibition by Brent Libraries. In 1982, Coventry's Minority Services Support Group (see organizations) published a pack for pupils about her. It was not until 1984 that her own splendid account *Wonderful Adventures of Mary Seacole in many lands* was re-issued in full, with valuable notes by the two Brent Library researchers, Ziggy Alexander and Audrey Dewjee. But in general books on the history of the period, she remains invisible.

Any review of a school's printed resources must take into account that the overall bias reflected in the collection as a whole, underpins and enhances biases in the hidden curriculum. Collectively, resources communicate a pervasive message to both students and teachers; the rest of this chapter examines in detail some specific issues.

1 Contingency responses

One outcome of child-centred education is that the early initiatives in multicultural education were in direct response to children in the classroom or school who, because of their ethnic or racial differences, had perceptibly different educational needs. The attitude: 'They're all the same to me', now condemned as racist, was in the

1960s and 1970s recognized by some teachers, often in isolation, as being of little help to those pupils. Individual teachers or, in a few cases, individual schools, began to rethink what they were teaching the pupils and often their first strategy was to seek new resources with which they could teach children something different. They inundated with questions the information services of organizations. Generally they wanted something specific; often the issues had not been thought through. Typical questions were:

There are two West Indian boys in my class – what can I give them to read?'
'Are there any books for children in Vietnamese/Pushto/ Hausa?'
'I suddenly looked at the kids in front of me and wondered what the assembly could mean to most of them: have you got anything multicultural I could use?'

Very occasionally there was a query for a book that would inform the teacher about the background of one or some of the children in the class.

In every case, the teacher was preparing to extend her own knowledge, curriculum and classroom strategy in direct response to a new, or newly perceived audience. The response was client-based.

It is no accident that the Association for Teaching English to Pupils from Overseas, (ATEPO) and later the National Association for the Teaching of English (NATE) were in the *avant-garde* of multicultural education. The arrival of bilingual children in schools necessitated developing teachers' professional competence so that they could assist children with their essential survival task of acquiring English, but the work of the pioneers extended to a recognition that the children might have cultural and educational needs of a special nature that went beyond the language issue. Because the organizations were addressing themselves also to issues of dialect, the special needs of children of West Indian origin also came under consideration.

The first schools which made re-adjustments along multicultural lines were the schools with large percentages of ethnic minority pupils. Teachers from these schools joined the National Association for Multiracial Education (NAME) and began the invaluable exchange of information, ideas and successful strategies. Teachers in all-white schools mostly saw it as no concern of theirs.

Due to a variety of philosophical, research and institutional and organizational pressures, these teachers are now being expected to accept, as part of their professional competence, the skill to educate their pupils for our multicultural society. Though this is an appropriate development, it may lead to a 'goldfish bowl' approach, as Edie Garvie (1983) calls it. This may take the form of children who are all followers of the dominant faith going to gawp at the Gurdwara, or the one Indian child in a class being asked about her sari or samosas. Unconsidered use of published resources can endorse this approach; great sensitivity is needed.

No child wants to be picked out as different, even if it is because she is 'special'. Parents and children have objected to this practice, which may be totally well-intentioned, but even books like the STRAND series (1978) can precipitate the situation in class where one child feels singled out or picked on; it is possibly the rarity value of such materials, and not their content, that is the cause. But child-centred education will be of far more benefit if it starts not from what the child is identified (by the dominant group) as *being*, but from what the child *knows*. Such an approach can be the basis of a strategy for the combat of bias, and will be considered further on in such a context.

2   The samosa syndrome

may also appear in cookery classes: Cornish pasties the norm; samosas what Asians eat. Whereas a re-assessed home economics curriculum would, in taking a multicultural approach, teach that chappattis and pitta, bagels and roti, pizzas and patties, are all varieties of bread, as staple (and as delicious) as a brown loaf or a baguette. Textile and handicrafts, dyeing and batik, can pay due acknowledgment to the geographic origins of design, as could Craft and Design Technology.

Once we are considering these subjects, mention must be made of:

3   Subject stereotyping by gender

The Schools Council's Sex Deferentiation in Schools Project examined schools in the light of differentiation by gender. The research all bears out the unsurprising fact that it is girls who do home economics and boys who do CDT in the *vast majority* of schools. It documents also the programmes that some schools are adopting to combat this sexism in curriculum options, but again books show only boys at the lathe and girls at the sewing machines or, equally inappropriately, the typewriter – which confirms attitudes for both pupils and curriculum planners, and makes it difficult for the individual pupils who do not cross the gender divide. One Schools Council publication that emanated from this study, *Pour out the Cocoa Janet* (1983) explores this in detail. There are, however, major efforts to change the situation particularly in the design and technology area. Two projects have examined the problems and have produced recommendations that are being widely implemented to schools. They are the Girls into Science and Technology Project and the Girls and Technological Education Project (GIST and GATE). Both are reviewed extensively in *Studies in Design Education Craft and Technology* (1983).

4 Biased attitudes of teachers

can be underpinned and given a specious authority by the biases in printed materials. This has already been touched on in relation to sport, but the racist and sexist assumptions made in books for teachers can pervade the ethos of the entire school. Much of the early writing about children from ethnic minorities presented *them* as the problem. Even a 1983 publication has been identified as having a 'strong assimilationist versus repatriation undertone' (Marina Foster 1983) and contributions by teachers and head-teachers like Ray Honeyford in the *Times Educational Supplement* (1984) still stress how awkward it is to have Asian pupils in the school.

This perception of black children as problematic can result in the whole ethos of the school being tainted by racism. It is likely that the teachers will have low expectations of the 'problem' children, which may not only curtail their examination options, but which will have a direct effect on the performance of these children. Research by Peter Green, summarized in Milner (1983) has shown the way in which 'ethnocentric' and 'non-ethnocentric' teachers (self-defined by a questionnaire) treat groups of children – white, Asian or West Indian, boys or girls, quite differently. The research illustrates also that children respond in accordance to this treatment – a conclusion that has implications for all adults working with children.

5 Examinations

will reflect the bias in textbooks in a rather different way. A chicken-and-egg process operates here: the resources are determined by the exam syllabus, but the examination questions are set according to the information available in the resources. This was intriguingly demonstrated by an incident in 1978. Clive Lawton, Education Officer of the Jewish Board of Deputies, enquired of the University of London Examinations Board why their Modern History syllabus did not set a question on a major event of the twentieth century: the Holocaust. The answer he received was that there were no resources on the subject. The shelves of personal accounts, poetry, novels, and the hard information in collections of contemporary documents, historical and statistical evidence and books of all sizes recording the events in Nazi Germany and the Reich in the 1930s and 1940s in the Board of Deputies' library belied the claim. Lawton, however, decided to accept that, with the exception of the work of Martin Gilbert (e.g. *The Atlas of the Holocaust* 1975) there was no book dealing with the massacres as a discrete subject for GCE students. A group of history teachers, RE teachers and historians, a few of them Jewish, set out to produce such a resource as a strategy for confounding the University. They were overtaken. In 1981, Tony Bayfield's *Churban: the murder of the Jews of Europe*, was published by the Michael Goulston Foundation. Now there was a children's book which, drawing largely on contemporary documents, gave a historical account of the social background and conditions in Germany in the 1930s, the propaganda and legislation that curtailed the lives of Jews and reduced them to 'untermenschen' (lesser humans), and the genocide that followed. It could not answer, but did not avoid, the inevitable question of how Germans allowed these atrocities to happen in their midst (one extraordinary teaching strategy for tackling this issue is written up in the form of a novel: *The Wave*, by Moreton Rhue (1982)). No longer could examination boards deny the existence of entirely appropriate resources.

A good deal more will have to be done to make changes at the level of examinations boards, but as a teacher at a recent conference observed: 'the Boards are, after all, made up of teachers: it is we who must make the changes'. NAME, the Commission for Racial Equality and advisers from Education Authorities around the country are pressuring the Boards. Educationists are also using a strategy that is known to succeed: whole new syllabuses are developed – along the lines of Nuffield Science or the Secondary Maths Project – that have built into them their own assessment programme. The Schools Council's Geography for the Young School Leaver was one such opportunity to eliminate the racism from the curriculum at examination level. It was an opportunity largely missed, according to the evaluation by Dawn Gill which

Schools Council chose not to publish in 1983 but which was summarized in *Multicultural Teaching* 1.1. (1983). GYSL, however, had offered the opportunity for a total re-evaluation of geography syllabuses.

6 Timetables

Even without the spectre of examinations, resources alone can determine the curriculum in an ethnocentric way that may go beyond the subject itself. Music textbooks were considered in Chapter 6; they provide a convenient illustration of problems of timetabling. Because they are excluded from the textbooks that dictate the curriculum, West Indian steel-pan or African drumming cannot readily be taught as part of the regular syllabus. So the strategy in multicultural education has been to offer lessons on these instruments as options. As we have seen, such strategies were initiated in multiracial and multicultural schools and, naturally, these options attracted mostly, or even only, black children. Whereas in primary schools all music can readily be taught to all the children, at secondary level 'options' mean that something else has to be left out. This left the schools, and the principles of 'multicultural education', wide open to attack. Farrukh Dhondy, Salman Rushdie and others have taken a swipe at multicultural education as 'banging a few bongo drums or how to tie a sari', and while this definition is quite contrary to what is understood by those working in the field of multicultural education, such objections in terms of who learns what in the schools is justified.

The most significant attack, on identical lines, has been that of Maureen Stone (1981). Again, many practitioners would disagree with the way she defines the term, for she does so in a narrow and partial way that makes it extremely easy then to demolish. But her attack on a practice of teaching black children African dance or hairstyles when their white classmates are progressing with their English, Maths or Physics, raises a crucial issue. If these 'multicultural' options are taught during the time when children should be working on a recognized 'classics-based' curriculum, which will teach them the skills that are recognized and valued in our society and which will lead to qualifications that may equip them for future jobs, then the entire practice can indeed be attacked as racist. Or as John Eggleston (1984) expresses it: 'Either way the minority ethnic group child loses, trading unmarketably low attainment in high status knowledge of the mainstream culture for unmarketable high status in low status knowledge of the minority culture.'

7 Biased teaching approaches

Even where there are no constraining exams, bias in the curriculum materials will produce biased teaching approaches – unless other materials are developed. Again with reference to the previous chapter, it may be illuminating to look at a mathematics curriculum in terms of the work by Ray Hemmings (1984).

Teaching counting is, according to many textbooks, done with bars and blocks, pencil and chalk only. Seldom with an abacus, and much later with a calculator. There are, however, children who know a highly sophisticated way of counting: by working along phalanges and knuckles, they can count on their fingers all the way to 1,000. They learned this in another culture – an Arabic one. Not only do teachers fail to pass on this splendid technique to all the children in the class, but due to their ignorance and the failure of books to enlighten them, they are likely to correct children when they see them using this technique. When teachers do this, it is under a misapprehension that the technique is 'childish': in fact they are undermining in the child an immensely useful skill.

8 Attitudes to languages other than English

The children's own languages and dialects need also to be recognized and valued by the school and in this area too, resources have an effect. Many pupils speak one or several dialects. Teachers are particularly aware of those from the Caribbean, accepting them less readily on the whole than those of, say Scotland. Dialects should be recognized in all schools for what they are: developed languages facilitating the full complexity of communication and with their own rules of syntax and grammar. No one dialect is 'superior' to another – not even the Standard English based on the dialect of Southern England. Certainly it is this form that is needed for all formal transactions, including interviews or answering examination questions, and a mastery of it is an advantage, so should be taught to all our children. But children operate along a continuum of dialect, adopting the appropriate form, often unconsciously. Many can also switch dialects to accommodate to their audience and circumstance: research for the Reading Through Understanding project (1976) discovered this to be quite commonplace among young black children, and quote as a typical case a five-year-old who had arrived with his family from Barbados three months earlier, spoke Bajan at home, approximated to Standard English in the classroom and was also operating in the London–Kingston that was the lingua franca of that school playground.

9   Attitudes to English

The Colonial Empire notion that English would be understood anywhere so long as one spoke loudly enough or in pidgin, and that the people who, through good grace or necessity, did attempt to respond in English, talked 'funny', is enshrined in a huge number of books. In such books, the English spoken by 'the natives' is standard-gone-wrong; every deviation is an error. The errors are not necessarily consistent; it is much more important that they be 'amusing', so inviting ridicule, or should illustrate the incompetence and ignorance of the characters – they cannot even speak properly. A splash of servility was often added:

In modern tales, black people are still shown to be struggling with the King's English as if pronunciation were a congenital defect. Not just third generation 'Sambo of the Snow Mountains' (de la Mare, 1977) who, when unable to tell why his 'Massa' wants a ticket to the Snow Mountains, says 'Me no know', but the language is loosely drawn from the Southern American dialect as spoken by slaves, so the speaker is further kept in his place. What is more, the native English speaking characters are not exposed by attempting to speak Hindi, Xhosa or whatever the language of the people may be, so their superiority is never undermined.

These attitudes to language and dialect are racist and misinformed. Projects such as Reading Through Understanding, the Linguistic Diversity Project (1980), a large body of research and books by Viv Edwards (1983), Peter Trudgill (1974) and many others endorse the early work of linguists in the US in confirming the sophisticated linguistic competence of dialect speakers. The Inner London Education Authority has produced its own booklets on dialect for teachers, and the issue is focused on in In-Service for language work and for multicultural education. Information alone, however, works exceedingly slowly on attitudes, and the bias in books has done a powerful job in debasing dialect.

There are enough published materials now available to overturn this bias. The Commission for Racial Equality and the National Association for Multiracial Education have featured the issue widely and Inner London's English Centre tackles the issues in its *English Magazine*, and in a booklet on dialect. They also produce the *Languages Book* (1981) for use in secondary classrooms. A spin-off from the Language Diversity Project, this is a superb presentation of languages and dialects as all of equal validity. Students working through the exercises will find that English is just one of a myriad of equally effective languages, and 'standard' only one of a considerable number of dialects.

There is also literature in dialects – to house in the library and use in the classroom. Such work demonstrates that dialects often have more to offer than 'standard' in expressing certain feelings and ideas. Accabra Huntley's little anthology of verse (1977) illustrated how a ten-year-old girl used 'standard' to write of her observations and experiences of her London life, and Guyanan dialect to explore her links with the Caribbean and her black identity. *City Lines* (1983) has other examples of emotive poetry in dialect by young people, so do the publications of the Afro-Caribbean Education Resource Project and *Black Ink* (see organizations). James Berry compiled a splendid anthology in *Bluefoot Traveller* (1981) and has, like John Agard, published collections of his own work. Some are featured also in the splendid *Caribbean Anthology* (1982), a pack contining not only books of poems by acknowledged poets such as John La Rose and Mervyn Morris, but cassettes in which they are read aloud, where possible by the poet, but always in appropriate dialect or accent. Students have been much inspired by the recordings of Linton Kwesi Johnson – *Dread, beat and blood* (1976) and *Englan' is a Bitch* (1980) who used dialect to rage against racism.

On a lighter note, accent and idiom that enhance expression dot the pages of Share-a-story with delight. Compare 'I haven't eaten for three days' with the way Anansi tells it: 'for three day the pot turn down'. These materials also feature cassettes, with a variety of Caribbean accents giving rhythms and cadences to the tales that make them leap to life. Some schools, both primary and secondary, have encounraged children to make their own attempts at writing in a chosen dialect, stimulating long discussions about the most accurately representative spelling; it was junior children who determined the spelling of the dialect passages in the *Reading through Understanding* book about Marcus Garvey. The teachers are not teaching dialects in place of standard – for most it would be presumptious, if not impossible. Also, it would, as black parents have made very clear, be to disadvantage their children. The object of studying dialect is to give the appropriate respect to the ways in which people speak, and to extend the understanding of English so that it is seen to be infinitely hospitable and flexible. Arguably, this contextualizing process can enhance students' command of standard forms. The approach: 'Standard would express it/spell it like this' avoids the bias inherent in approaches and materials that assert: 'this is the right way'.

10 The language hierarchy

Resources often suggest a language hierarchy, with English at the top, European languages led by French and German next, and community languages, especially those like Sylheti with no specific literature, at the bottom. The *Languages Book* (1981) debunks this approach too, and teachers will find much guidance from the publications of the Lingusitic Minorities Project (1984) and the Schools Council Mother-Tongue Project and the Bilingual Under-Fives Project (BUF). The principle of validating home languages is not new: Bullock was published in 1975, and it states unequivocally: 'No child should be expected to cast off the language and culture of the home as he (sic) crosses the school threshold, and the curriculum should reflect those aspects of his life'.

Certain processes militate against a high status for community languages in schools. Children themselves recognize that English is the language they will need for survival at school and in society, and teachers may be so anxious to support and encourage their learning of it that they give the impression that the child's first language is of little account. It is very likely that the teacher will speak not a word of that language if it is not European; in many cases, teachers have not even ascertained what the language of the child *is*. This leads to cases being recorded of children refusing to speak the home language even to their mothers. Our language is a significant part of our identity – such a devaluing is potentially damaging to the child's self-image. It can also actually impede cognitive development in children up to the age of six (see J. Wright, 1983).

The National Council for Mother Tongue Teaching plus other bodies, projects and Local Education Authorities, are now developing a programme of mother-tongue maintenance and teaching as part of the curriculum. There are still very few schools with timetabled lessons in language such as Turkish, Cantonese, Gujerati, Punjabi, Bengali, and they, too, have the problem of how to timetable these options without reducing the opportunities for academic study.

Resources, however, can play a major part in offsetting the bias against community languages. If children see books in a range of languages, including their own, on the shelves in the reading corner and library, the school is saying something very important to them.

It is recognizing the languages of bilinguals and endorsing them with their approval. It matters little whether or not the bilingual children can read the books; they will certainly recognize the script. And if the books are borrowed and read to the children by parents, they too will receive the school's message about their language; as much as when, more practically, school letters and notices are sent to the family in appropriate languages.

My argument can be underlined by my observations of the children from over fifty schools who attended *Storytime at CUES*, in 1976. This was an exhibition of books in eight community languages (with readers to open the books to the children at scheduled times). There were children from six to thirteen and in each of the language groups who had believed up until then that all storybooks were in English. Their faces glowed when they saw and handled books in their home languages that were clearly intended, with their pictures, bright colours and large scripts, for *them*. A simple lesson, but clearly a profound óne – and a useful lesson for native English speakers too, that books are not their prerogative.

Where they can be found, books in all the languages spoken by the school population should be on the shelves of the library and anywhere else that is appropriate. It is not an expensive exercise – most of the materials from South East Asia, China and the India sub-continent are very cheap indeed – but it is demanding, even daunting. Most Indian and some other books have English versions that allow for assessment, but in many cases, it is the members of that linguistic group, drawn from the parents and local groups, on whose judgment teachers will have to rely for selecting the books.

11 The school library

I shall end this chapter where I began it: in the school library. As well as books in community languages, there could be shelf labels and guides in appropriate languages, so that the materials can be readily found. Posters, notices and even the short guide to the catalogue or indexing system – the one that ends: 'if yoú can't find what you want, ask the Librarian', can easily be translated into appropriate languages. For even in this age of attractive and welcoming school libraries, where pot plants have replaced the portraits of past headteachers, and paperbacks and periodicals are relevant to the interests of the pupils, it is still all too easy to give out a subtle message that the library is only for the English speakers, or the studious, or the middle classes. Or, as has already been suggested, that only certain subjects, certain people and certain cultural, racial and linguistic groups are of any account.

12 Classification schemes

Even when the range of materials is extended in ways considered under 'Selection Procedures', their *arrangement* may reflect biases both racist and sexist.

The Library of Congress scheme (more widely employed in the USA), until recently listed 'abortion' under the heading 'MURDER'. In the UK all public and most school libraries are organized according to the Dewey Decimal Classification.

There are evidences of both racism and sexism in Dewey, and no doubt at all about its monocentricism (Anglo–Americans, to be precise). For example, out of the ten main classes, the 200s is devoted to religion – of this, 228–89 deals only with Christianity. One tenth, from 290–9, has to cover all other religions, including Buddhism and Islam, each with more followers than Christianity, and with Judaism, Hinduism, Jainism. As for Taoism, Confucianism and Shintoism, they are tagged on simply as 'other religions'. Language (400s) and literature (800s) follow a similar pattern with 420–89 concerned with European languages only, and the same amount of space (490s) given to all other languages, as is given to English alone (420s). There is little the librarian can do to counter these imbalances, short of rewriting the classification scheme, which is certainly not to be recommended. As well as being aware of the biases, however, there are certain aspects of Dewey to which she could pay particular attention:

(a) *Terminology*

Derogative terms have been expunged from later editions of Dewey, but certain out-dated descriptions are still reflected as in the descriptors for 301.44: 'hobos, tramps, untouchables, hippies'.

(b) Position

The classification system's objective is not only to bring together all materials on the same subject, but also to bring related topics close together. In terms of ethnic minorities, Dewey fails on both counts.

The librarian has to decide whether she wants, for example, to have everything about the Caribbean grouped together, or whether Caribbean cookery should stay with Cookery (which would be my view). An effective way of overcoming this is to cross-reference in the index, so that a reader who does want a range of information on the Caribbean will find a reference to the 640s, Cookery, under the section on the Caribbean, or guides in the subject index.

Where there are regular requests for information covering a wide range of topics, a printed bibliography of the relevant materials available in the library is a useful solution, so long as these are either updated or abandoned before they become inaccurate.

(c) *Arrangement*

No librarian need arrange her materials in strict Dewey order – books can be pulled out of all ten classes and set together, either as a temporary display or as a permanent collection if that is the way they will be required and used.

For all its inadequacies, Dewey is flexible, infinitely expandable due to its decimal pattern, and regularly updated to incorporate new or developing areas of knowledge. It is also the scheme used in almost all public libraries in the UK, so that a child soon learns that he will find material on Ancient Egypt at 932 in school and public library alike, and gains confidence in using both. For these reasons, it seems unavoidable to continue to classify libraries by Dewey.

(d) *Labels and guides*

These should be absolutely clear, so that there is no mystique about how materials are arranged in the library. Headings should relate to the school curriculum rather than the Dewey classes – a heading, for example, for HINDUISM, even if it is a tiny sub-section of Dewey, if comparative religion is studied in the school. Again, attention should be paid to terminology, and labels in other languages may be appropriate (especially for the collections in mother-tongues themselves). Clear instructions on use of the indexes and catalogue, a large, bright, simplified index, again relating to both clientele and curriculum, is likely to be much used and may be worth translating into languages appropriate to the school.

Conclusions

Identifying and analysing the racist bias in specific examples of curriculum materials is of little value in itself, and has been dismissed by some educational practitioners as nitpicking. But in the context of a re-evaluation of the whole school's practice: *what* is taught, how and why, it can be of considerable value. An understanding of the issues underlying the bias of one particular book can sharpen the awareness of teachers. They can move on to a consideration of the overall messages contained in the school's resources and, further, to how it determines their own teaching.

Tokenist materials support tokenist curriculum modifications; two typical examples from the 1970s are steel bands and slavery. Teaching about such topics was all that teachers were called on to do. They did not have to consider their own racist acceptance of the hierarchy of knowledge as laid down by the curriculum and its resources. They did not have to confront their own assumptions and expectations of pupils in relation to the pupils' race, sex and class; assumptions which often deterimined which students took 'O' level in maths, which took cookery and which a Mode III Black Studies course. The examinations perpetuate the defined parameters of knowledge and the hierarchy of knowledge, the text books have been written in response to those examination syllabuses and further legitimate their defined areas of worthwhile knowledge.

The resources used generally in the school are a reflection of the attitudes and values of the staff and, in their turn, serve also to underpin and fix those attitudes and values. The vicious circle is visible in the school library, or for that matter the public library; clearly displayed is the range of knowledge deemed worthy of study and thus of perpetuation, by the institution. But the library is ideally suited to extending the parameters of perceptibly valid knowledge far beyond the school curriculum. This seldom happens. The library stock, the artwork, posters and other materials on display generally serve to institutionalize the cultural hierarchy of knowledge. The dominant culture's publications continue to dominate.

Chapter 8

Strategies for combat I: sanitize or sensitize?

Once it is accepted that books and resources do shape attitudes, and that many project pejorative biases, the question becomes: what can be done about it? This chapter is devoted to the resources already present in schools; the next will look at possible future acquisitions.

That resources be re-evaluated in the light of bias has been recommended by organizations and publications since the 1970s. Bullock (1975) identified as meriting 'urgent attention', 'the nature of the reading material that is used in schools. In their verbal representation of society, and in their visual content, books do a great deal to shape children's attitudes. We would urge that teachers and librarians should have this in mind when selecting books for schools'.

Authorities like Bedfordshire, Inner London and Haringey alerted schools to the potential damage of biased books in schools and the Library Association and teacher unions acknowledged the importance of the issue. The National Union of Teachers examined the issue of racial stereotyping in books in a 1979 publication: *In black and white*. There were also firm recommendations for the removal of offensive material, such as Rampton (1981), quoted in Chapter 1.

Hard on Rampton's heels came the Scarman Report (1981), which endorsed Rampton's views on education and resources. The Home Affairs Committee Report (1981) stated: 'We are concerned that some older textbooks, in particular at primary school levels still reflect racial attitudes now discredited and we expect local authorities to act with suitable vigour to have these withdrawn'.

Implicit in the wording of many of these statements is a recognition that the issue is not straightforward. The convenient word 'replace', in the sense of removing the bad book and putting in its place a good one, is either naive or a cop-out. Books do not come in perfect pairs, both with identical subject matter and for the same age level, and with one clearly pejoratively biased and the other benign.

Simplisitic approaches are likely to evoke a response usually expressed as follows: 'If we take all the books that are class-biased, racist or sexist off the shelves, there will be nothing left'. This statement, too, is too facile to be wholly true, but it is a reaction worth noting because it gives permission to do nothing at all, merely to continue as before. It often masks a strong resistence on the part of the speaker to the notion that she or he should be actively concerned with issues of equality in education.

It is true that once we begin to remove biased books from the shelves – and it *will* be removal, not replacement – the shelves may begin to look rather bare. How bare brings us on to the next set of differences: how strong does the negative bias have to be before the book qualifies for elimination?

There is no arbitrary pass-or-fail mark against which we can measure books in such terms. In fact the fate of individual publications will depend ultimately upon *who* in the school identifies and quantifies the bias. Decisions have been taken, however, along pragmatic lines, which have cleared collections of the most offensive materials. It may be useful to explore some of the issues in detail:

Who decides?

In organizations with a commitment to equality of education, the answer is generally: several people. It may be in informal consultation – with colleagues in the school, with pupils and parents, and possibly with outside agencies, such as multicultural advisers, librarians, local Community Organizations or in response to the influence of published criticism. Or there may be a more formal strategy, such as a working party made up of teachers and, if there is one, the librarian, who address themselves to the demanding task of sorting through the stock. This formal structure has much to recommend it: it facilitates the sharing of responsibility, and the opportunity to bring to the attention of all the school staff the importance of bias in materials.

As a strategy for the combating of racism in schools, such a re-examination of resources is recommended in practically all published policies on educational equality as being part of the overall re-evaluation of educational objectives, policy and curriculum in the school. In some schools which have not yet addressed themselves to this overall task, starting with the resources has been a catalyst. School librarians have gathered some of the most racist books from their shelves and, instead of discreetly withdrawing them, brought them to their teacher colleagues. This has in some cases led to an initial alerting of staff to the reality of racism within their school.

Similarly, resources can offer an oblique approach to anti-racism in in-service courses. The concerned minority who sign up for race awareness training will at least be prepared to acknowledge that racism, sexism and prejudice are a reality of society and of our schools: it is the unaware or dismissive majority who need to be taken on. It is hopeless to tell them that society, and much of education, is racist and sexist; more counterproductive still to suggest that *they* are racist or sexist. The two most predictable responses are – (1) 'the others maybe but not me', or (2) 'I feel that we should all go home and just slit our throats' (overheard after a harangue by an angry academic to the whole staff of a secondary school).

Pointing out the racism and sexism in *children's books* in the context of in-service training is far less threatening. The audience is not responsible for the production of those materials, nor are its members even being exposed for using them. A recurring response is 'I never thought about that before'. A small beginning, but still a beginning, may have been made. Immediate further support can be offered in the form of advice on what resources may be more appropriate, and information about the support and further guidance available: advisory services, organizations, local consultative collections of resources, publications to extend teachers' knowledge on the issues.

Whoever decides what to discard and what to keep, on what are their decisions based? Criteria for evaluation of children's materials are readily available and the most accessible and widely-used have been described in Chapter 2. Better still is the development of criteria in relation to the resources under review, but in the end, the decisions will be tempered by a range of variables – just as will *all* selection of books for children by adults: a preference for the familiar, a half remembered favourable review, evidence of the response evoked by a book in a child, the general 'knowledge' of who is and who is not a good author, the selections displayed in teachers' centres, libraries, resource centres, and, of course, the content of the book. And, ultimately, how the selectors themselves feel about the degree of bias in the book.

To these vague and interrelated determinants can be added some sharper considerations:

    (i)   Is there anything else on the subject at that level?
    (ii)   Does the book make a unique and valuable contribution in its field?
    (iii)   Who is the book for?
    (iv)   How will it be used?

Just as women gain strength from finding their experience documented in books, be these novels or sociological reports, black people welcome accounts of their experience, and this will, in the US or the UK, inevitably include experience of racism: it is how it is expressed that matters.

David Buckingham (1984) has argued that stereotyping is not a simple issue and that the substitution of 'positive' stereotypes for 'negative' ones is not the answer. The negative stereotype is the dominant one; the one perpetuated by the dominant group for the dominated, for it 'derives from a consensus, fitting with the end power relations of society (whereas) "positive images" do not. They derive from a critical stance towards that ideology and that consensus . . . and may be a form of "wishful thinking", a representation of things as they might be and not as they are'.

To comment thus far: this 'wishful thinking' is often rather more in the case of feminist strategy: deliberate role reversal is an effective way of getting people to think about the unrealistic basis on which stereotypes of women are based, as a first step to challenging them. But this does not work for racism for, as Buckingham points out, the 'positive images' may be too easily refuted as 'not like that' or, more seriously, that they portray only a partial reality. 'In this society', he avers, 'it remains a fact that very few women, black people or working class people attain powerful positions' and books that show them in such positions are doing nothing to overturn the racism in society: they may even be sustaining it. Once more we ask, 'whose interests do such images serve – for whom are such stereotypes "positive"?' He continues: 'Images of black people which show them being assimilated into a white society may be reassuring for liberal white people, but they may also detract from the unique strength and identity of black cultures, and draw attention away from continuing inequality and injustice.' He goes further still: 'If "positive images" are based on a pretence that oppression and discrimination do not exist, then they are clearly dangerous.'

Nor, he argues, can it ever be assumed that an anti-racist text will assuredly produce an anti-racist response – this, too, is wishful thinking.

Buckingham has made the point powerfully and fully in relation to media images, but I cannot resist taking the debate a little further still and in relation to children's books, although I suspect that to develop it extensively would not be appropriate here. So I shall be brief: the 'positive images' can become the *raison d'etre* for children's books to be written and published in the UK 'out of something called conscience or something less enlightened called commerce'. The words I am now quoting are those of Farrukh Dhondy who attacks these books in an article (1983) 'The appropriate slant'. One example he cites is from a book which includes a story about the hygienic procedures in the lavatory; the rest are about food and customs. My own reasons for rejecting this manuscript was that I could see no reason that children would want to read these stories. Literature is not social therapy, nor do children read stories because they are good for them.

Children, like adults, should find their motivation for reading literature within the literature itself. The novels of Rushdie, Desai, Jhabvala have no connection whatever with the formula books which show Asian characters, doing 'ordinary' things that will 'supposedly assert a benign influence on the future of Britain'. As Dhondy expresses it: 'they live in the world of Booker prizes, to be literature, not to fulfil a socio-political educational need, and have only very marginally been adopted as required reading for sixth forms.' Books written to be literature are the only ones from which children have anything to gain. Such books for children are, as Dhondy asserts, pretty thin on the ground. We should be looking for more like *The Borribles go for broke* by Michael de Larrabeiti 'in which a Bangladeshi Borrible by the name of Twilight (note, not even Twilight-Miah or Sunset-Ullah) shares the geography and mythology of the regular Borribles . . . a perfect literary vehicle for integration (of myth and reality)' and what all books worth reading should offer.

Classroom texts

Even a biased book can be used to some good purpose in the classroom, so long as the teacher has control over how it is used and is alert to the bias within it. Teachers need to recognize their responsibility as agents between their pupils and the books: they are automatically endorsing the materials with their own implicit approval unless they specifically say otherwise and indicate the passages with which they disagree.

The books placed on shelves for children to read on their own, for their private study or for leisure, require closer scrutiny. There will not be a librarian, teacher or parent present to act as a buffer between the child and the book. The age of the readers is another determining variable: encouraging children to challenge what they read is a major strategy which will be discussed in detail in the following pages, but the younger the child, the more generally accepting – and impressionable – they are.

To date most decisions about withdrawal of biased books have been to replace what is replaceable and to discard the books that misinform and mislead, since if they are not dangerous they are at best pointless. Also dispensible are works like *Here comes Golly* (see p. 41), the High-Low readers, or Blyton's *Story of the little black doll* (who becomes recognizably loveable after being left out in the rain). No child's imaginative experience will be the poorer if they are deprived of such storybooks; but the same cannot be said of the works of Sarah Gertrude Millin or Kipling. However, literature of this enduring quality needs to be presented to young people in the context of the attitudes that prevailed at the time it was written.

The elimination from the shelves of all books and materials that are biased is totally unrealistic, but would it even be desirable? A totally sanitized collection of resources would be so out of touch with reality as to be of little use to the pupils. Prejudice is a reality of their lives and cannot be wholly expunged from their literature.

The most effective and lasting strategy for combating racism and sexism and other damaging bias in books is to teach children to challenge everything they read. They need to learn to doubt the messages of the media and to develop and ultimately to trust their own judgment. This cannot be taught in a single lesson, nor even in a term. A healthy scepticism for the apparent authority of print and a real respect for the children's own experience so that it is brought to bear on their learning, has to be a powerful and continuing dimension of the visible and hidden curriculum. The remainder of this chapter is devoted to this key objective: some specific strategies that have been found effective are here described.

1   *Asking questions*

Teachers should challenge the bias in books as it is encountered:

'Do you think that's true? Why should the author have said that. . . .?' There are also more precise questions to be asked; ideally teachers and pupils should devise their own checklists in given subject areas. A valuable model of how deeply such analysis can probe is provided by Hicks (1981). It develops from one central and crucial question: 'Why are poor countries poor?'

(i) *Causes* – Is it assumed or suggested that there is only one cause of poverty? If so, is this diagnosed as being largely due to over-population or to environmental restraints with no consideration of economic factors?

(ii) *State* – Is underdevelopment considered to be a state or a set of conditions which people just happen to find themselves in and therefore need to get out of?

(iii) *Process* – Is it suggested that underdevelopment can also be explained as an historical process which arises out of the unequal relationship between rich and poor countries?

(iv) *Today* – Is it shown that such unequal relationships still persist today and that neo-colonialism may continue to hinder development?

(v) *Catching up* – Is there an assumption that 'third world' countries need to catch up with richer countries and that development is to be equated with economic growth alone?

(vi) *Choices* – Is it shown that there are choices over models of development and that different models are in favour at different times and in different places?

(vii) *Concept* – Is the concept of development also discussed in relation to the satisfaction of basic needs and non-material needs?

(From *Bias in Geography Texts*, 1981)

For children to learn to doubt the messages of the media, to develop and ultimately to trust their own judgment, teachers have to have gone through a similar process first. For pupils this crucial learning experience has to be a powerful and continual dimension of the visible and hidden curriculum.

2 *Demystifying print*

We have already considered how the process of learning to read usually involves a verification of what is read. If this process is not checked, the result is adults who believe everything they read – or read only what they wish to believe, choosing their daily newspaper, for instance, accordingly. There appears to be no documentation of work at the level of initial literacy acquisition that will undermine this process while actually teaching reading, but there are primary schools which at least undermine the apparent irrefutable authority of books by eliminating some of the mystique.

Side-by-side with the volumes of the mainstream publishers are displayed books written by the children themselves, or by adults they know well. One East End of London infant school invites parents and the community to compose stories for their children, in the home language. The author may also illustrate the story, or this may be done by the children. A technician then laminates and binds the books to a high standard of attractiveness and sturdiness, and onto the classroom and library shelves they go – a range of languages, orthography, opinions, all open to examination.

A junior school – in an all-white area and with a commitment to multicultural education – processes some of the writings of its pupils in a similar way. This school is open-plan, oriented around a central library collection to which children make constant reference, and from which they borrow extensively for leisure reading. There is a conventional catalogue, and *all* authors are entered, including the pupils; so yet another sacred authority has been made accessible.

Young children's writing is also increasingly enshrined in more established publications; such as the anthology of verse by primary children *Hey butterfly* (1976) and more and more material is appearing. It is notable also that the writers themselves do not usually come from the social group that produces most adult authors of children's books.

At secondary level it is even easier to make published writing the potential province of students. Some of the outcomes directly reflect the multicultural society, such as the English Centre's *Our lives* and *City lines* and the publications of Black Ink, already mentioned.

One teacher who set out to validate his students' own experiences and observations and encouraged them to commit their views and accounts to print was Chris Searle in *The world in a classroom* (1977). None of his students is likely to kneel at the altar of printed authority again, and the book is an excellent source from which to stimulate other students. Schools like Vauxhall Manor in London are inviting students to attempt to write in dialect as part of their study of English, so that language as well as viewpoints become more diverse and yet all part of the empire of print.

3 *Challenging the media*

in a more direct way has been a strategy developed mainly at secondary level. One resource which has been found useful is the Thames TV booklet *Viewpoint 2* (1981). Andrew Bethell wrote it to accompany four School TV programmes. He invited students to look critically at how four groups of people are portrayed by the media: Youth, Race, Workers and people on Welfare. By the time students have identified how inaccurately the media present *them*; that the stereotype they project of youth is far removed from what they know to be the reality, the students are ready to move on to the issue of race in the media. In this project, too, the students are invited to rewrite the scenario, representing individuals and groups more accurately. In another school, the sixth form examined prejudice among themselves and in society and their resulting video '*Why prejudice*' was broadcast by BBC.

4 *Teaching race relations in the classroom*

is a strategy being taken on in some schools. This has opened yet another debate: does a programme of lessons on race necessarily diminish racism? The findings so far have not been all that encouraging. Teachers are referred to NARTAR and the work of Lawrence Stenhouse, particularly to his *Teaching race relations; problems and effects* (1982) and to Klein (1984): *Race relations in the classroom: rationale and resources*.

Justice cannot be done to this large issue here, but two aspects are particularly relevant to our study. First, no programme on race relations for schools can fail to address itself to the issue of bias in books and the media. Second, sweeping racism under the carpet will not make it go away: the first step in combating it is taken by acknowledging its existence, whether in society at least, in housing, employment or education specifically, or in print and the media. This is argued with exemplary clarity in a video made by and available from ALTARF entitled: *Racism: the 4th R* (1983).

5 *Protesting*

to the creators of biased books is one strategy illustrated in the ALTARF video. At an inner London primary school, one class took exception to a little book on swimming, not because of its content, but because the illustrations, in an attempt to be multiracial, has some of the figures coloured grey. It was agreed by this class that no people are that colour, and a letter of objection went to the publishers, Dinosaur. They replied offering an explanation that it was done not to offend, but for reasons of cost. But the children, black and white, *were* offended. The next step was taken by the teacher: she photographed the class swimming at the local baths. The resulting pictures were then made by the children into their own book on swimming, a book which they all consider rather better than the one from Dinosaur, and certainly a book that portrays children, particularly black children, more accurately. It is illogical to compare the two works; the point is that a group of children who did not like what was on offer sought, and in this case, *made* an alternative.

It may take some time before these isolated acts of protest have much effect on publishers, although there is evidence that certain of them are taking note and this will be discussed further in relation to new materials. Children who have, with the support of teachers or other adults, registered an objection to a book with its publisher, will have learnt that they are not just tilting at windmills. Educational publishers cannot afford to ignore their market, and even if their replies are defensive and unsatisfactory, reply they must. In the end, it is their apparent infallibility that has been challenged. They are no longer perceived by their challengers as the ultimate authority on the suitability of material for inclusion in a book.

This is not to say that protest should not also have as its aim effecting change. In some cases it has achieved change: the Oompah Loompahs of the perennially popular *Charlie and the chocolate factory* have been changed from their original 'savage' form, though they are still *untermenschen*. Penguin withdrew its well-intentioned but disastrously conceived Primary Education Project within two years of its publication in 1974, and there are a number of other examples of modification or abandonment by publishers. And even if the number of titles in each house so affected may appear too small to be of consequence, the publishers themselves are being sensitized to the fact that their consumers object to pejorative bias in books. Whether the letters come in from individuals, institutions or groups, whether from parents, children, librarians or teachers, no publisher can afford to disregard them.

6   *Comparison of texts*

can be an effective strategy. Bias is so strong in books that 'facts' may, in two publications, appear totally contradictory. For example:

> The first Crusade . . . was the result of an appeal for Western help from the hard-pressed Emperor Alexius of Byzantium. His territories in Asia Minor had been captured by the Moslems in 1071, and the Saljuk's spreading power had put paid to the relatively peaceful relations he had enjoyed with the Arab occupiers of Palestine . . . He was attracted by the idea of getting foreigners to recapture his territories for him.

(from *The Invaders* by M. Windrow, 1979). Compare this with *The Crusades* by V. Bailey and E. Wise – Longmans, undated, 197?, where the following appears:

> About 900 years ago, the Christian pilgrims met trouble in the Holy Land. They were cruelly treated by the Saracens who had conquered Jerusalem. This made Christian people everywhere very angry. Alexius sent to the Head of the Christian Church, Pope Urban II, for help against the Saracens.

The viewpoints of the two authors are so opposed that if we accept what the one asserts, we cannot fully accept the other. While a demonstration of a similar kind, taken from newspaper reports, may be quite dramatically effective in the short term, given as part of a course on race relations, media studies etc., the most effective strategy is to make the point in the context of the curriculum at all levels in the school, as in the above example from history, and as often as possible. History and geography texts are likely to produce the most obviously conflicting statements, and notes of such examples could be circulated within departments. If there is a working party already re-assessing textbooks and resources, noting examples as they are encountered will be useful for the future. If there is a librarian in the school, she may be able to contribute to the collection. She should also be alert to opportunities to present and point out conflicting information and opinions in books when students consult her for their project work and private study.

7   *The librarian*

who is no more than a caretaker in a sanctuary, creates an impression of the sanctity of the books, their inviolable authority. The library can, however, play an active role in combating bias in books, but only if certain conditions prevail.

(i)   The librarian's professional parity with the teachers must be beyond question, and her special skills of information storage and retrieval recognized as useful – and available – to the rest of the staff.

(ii)   Opportunities for contact with colleagues should be guaranteed as part of the general organization of the school. However well a librarian maintains her collection, she will make little contribution to the educational objectives of the school if she is not part of relevant working parties, does not attend the staff meetings and INSET courses that reflect her concerns, is not active in the extra-curricular activities of the school. It is essential that she is not shackled to the library and that she is seen as an active agent for learning in the school.

(iii)   There should be space in the library for talking: if this is impossible, then there will need to be a good deal of *time* allowed (so limiting the opportunity for silent study). It must provide a venue for the sharing of ideas: students should be encouraged to discuss the resources among themselves, and the library should never have to double as a sin-bin.

(iv)   The librarian should keep informed about the content of her stock, so that she is able to discuss the books with the pupils (as in the example in Chapter 5) in an informal way.

(v)   The librarian can make an effective contribution to combating racism and sexism not just in books but in the school, in her role as information agent to the staff. She has to hand the resources and the skills that will enable her to keep informed about new developments in multi-cultural and anti-sexist education. The Fawcett Library's *Bibliofem* and *Multicultural Education Abstracts* are just two examples, both valuably specialized, among many that index relevant articles in journals. The librarian also has the opportunity to scan publications as they arrive and, if she has been kept aware of the curriculum and educational objectives of the teachers, she will be able to put into their hands the literature concerning new developments, so extending their own professional competence.

Like the teachers, the librarian has an active role in developing study skills in all the pupils in the school, in all subjects and in all years. If children's study skills have been developed to the full during their schooling, then practitioners will have truly equipped their pupils for learning. This must of necessity be the prime objective of education and it has implications for the issue of bias in books.

8 *Study skills*

There is no one perceived body of knowledge for transmission in schools to the next generation. The knowledge explosion has made such an approach impossible, even were it desirable. Add to this what Beswick (1977) calls 'the information explosion': the vast range of literature and media information sources now available, plus the facilities for easy and economical development of ephemeral resources. Thus any attempt at limiting the parameters of knowledge will necessarily be overwhelmed and much knowledge, in order to be of any use, has to be current: in many spheres, new knowledge replaces old and at a frenetic rate.

With these conditions operating, educationists should, as a pedagogical principle, be aiming to equip pupils to find the information they need in order to acquire the skills and knowledge that they want. It should be a central task of all active teaching agents – which includes classroom teachers and librarians – and wherever they succeed, they will have equipped their students also to identify and challenge bias in books and information sources. This is likely to be the most significant single strategy for combating bias in books. Developing students' own evaluative skills is part of the process of developing study skills and developing study skills is possible only if constantly taught as part of the curriculum, and in the context of each subject studied. With these skills to hand and a knowledge that a range of information tools is available to them, pupils are in a position to learn for themselves. They then are ready to *think* for themselves. Once pupils can locate materials for themselves, they will be faced with the need to select from what they find on the subject. Librarians and teachers have a significant role, one which has considerable implications for multicultural education, in teaching pupils to evaluate materials for their accuracy and perspective. The first step, which should be taken when they are providing resources, is to make their readers aware that they should not believe everything they read – perhaps by offering books with opposing views, and pointing this out to their clientele. The same wariness is needed by the teaching staff, to use in the classroom in the same way, supplying books with contradictory views to the textbooks, to be referred to in lessons.

Next, we need to assist readers in developing their own evaluation skills, suggesting some points for them to consider e.g. the date of the books, who the author is, whether there is a propaganda motive (show them an example, such as the glossy publications of the South African government), whether what is merely opinion is presented as hard factual information. This advanced work in 'study skills' is, I believe, central to the issue of publications in relation to the multicultural society and needs to be part of a wider programme in the school.

Conclusions

While we take heed of the recommendations of various significant bodies and publications to re-examine the books and resources used by and for children, it is seldom possible to replace the offensive ones and not always appropriate to withdraw them. What is most useful is the process of re-examination of materials, so that there is heightening awareness among the adults who mediate these resources. It can even be a relatively non-threatening way of raising the whole issue of racism in organizations such as schools and libraries.

There must be debate, and decisions should be a shared outcome, based on a consideration of who the book is for and how it will be used. In some circumstances, very negatively biased materials can be used in the classroom to raise issues for discussion. In the case of library books and fiction, we should continue to extend children's imaginations and experience through what they read, not offer reductions down to the mundane or even to quasi-factual descriptions of different customs offered in place of narrative. Enduring literature which reflects the biases of its time and place of writing should, however, be set in context for readers.

Most of our energies need to be directed not at what is read but at the young people reading it. They need to be first taught and then constantly encouraged to develop their own evaluative skills and not to believe without question everything they read. This can and should be done from very early in their school life and needs to be constantly reinforced throughout it; it is a prime 'study skill' which can be learned in context of all areas of the curriculum. What we should be working towards is a population whose 'literacy' goes beyond the transference of the symbols on the page to the recesses of the mind without any intermediate thought process. Only when that is made to happen will intellectual freedom become a reality.

Chapter 9

Strategies for combat II: censorship or selection?

Even if resources are being acquired for a school in which every student has been equipped to recognize and challenge bias in materials – should such a school exist – there seems to be little point in buying new stock loaded with blatant pejorative bias.

In practice, librarians, teachers and heads who are concerned about bias in materials, consider it part of their selection procedure to avoid doing so. They are in pursuit of excellence – and racist or sexist books simply do not come up to standard. However, there is another argument. What right have librarians to decide what the young population may or may not read? A sanitized view of the world is unrealistic and misleading; the librarian should ensure that all views should be fairly represented. It has to be said that even in the collections of school librarians who adopt this position, copies of *Mein Kampf, Did six million really die?* or hard pornography are not visible on the shelves.

Such debate serves chiefly to obfuscate the central issue, and has been angrily attacked by Christine Shawcroft, a school librarian (1983).

> There have been enough studies to convince of the damage done to the self-esteem of non-white middle class male children when they are continually confronted with derogatory stereotyped images. There has been enough research to demonstrate that certain expectations – say that girls can't do maths and science, that black kids are athletic, not academic – become self-fulfilling prophecies. But the research findings will get nowhere near the children as long as the impulse to block out challenges of complexity and of change can be camouflaged by the deliberate use of this emotive term – 'Censorship'.

No censorship, she argues, will mean no decisions, and discussion and decisions must continue. For, as Phil Goodall has observed (1982) 'as consumers, children are largely powerless . . . the adult purchaser, whether individual or institutional, makes the primary selections'. A responsibility not to be shirked.

The foundation of the 'who are we to say' debate becomes shakier still when we impose three weighty realities upon it. If it is good material that we are seeking to make available to students, many of the most derogatory publications are simply unacceptable. Second, there is no chance of stocking everything published as though a children's library or school collection were a copyright library: choices are being made all the time. Finally, in a school it is axiomatic that the materials in classrooms and library should serve the school.

Selection should, in fact, be closely identified with the educational aims and objectives of the school. Library stock too, should both serve these objectives and reflect them. Whether it is a teacher who has responsibility for the library or a chartered librarian, selection of stock will not be taking place in a vacuum, but in relation to the curriculum and the clientele of the school.

Before we leave the emotive issue of censorship, it is worth drawing attention to Zimet's (1976) excellent chapter 'Censorship and intellectual freedom'. She observes that while the ground for censorship will vary in different communities (to which I would add: and among people with different ideologies) there are many censors; parents, librarians, educational administrators and teachers, church groups and government officials and children themselves. Nevertheless, the most serious threat to intellectual freedom is precensorship: authors and publishers restricting their choice of content to the most acceptable, which means also the most econimically safe; textbook publishers particularly, Zimet observes, will be likely to stick to successful formulae, rejecting work that doesn't 'fit'.

Who selects?

Though in the end it is the librarian who does develop and determine the content of the collection, the resources of the library should be the concern of all the staff. The librarian must assume overall responsibility for not only maintaining and organizing but also determining the library, and will inevitably place the stamp of her own personality on it after a time. She cannot be responsible for the content of all the resources in the collection, and she should receive formal as well as informal support in selecting new stock. In relation to subject materials in schools, the issue is more clearcut. Teachers accept more readily their role in determining what resources are appropriate to their pupils, because they select them in relation to the curriculum. This approach holds for background reading and project materials as well as for textbooks. In selecting resources for, say, geography, they to some extent define and limit the parameters of geography in the school. They will also be influencing the attitudes that may be formed by the users of the resources. To ensure that this potential for influence and control be put to maximum beneficial effect, the school will need to develop an overall policy for the selection of all the resource materials, wherever they may be stored in the school. Sorting out the issues of bias in the materials in the context of one department or curriculum area can have only limited value – a schizoid approach will be avoided in a school that educates its students for a multicultural society and contributes to equality in society. Similarly, a separate selection policy for librarians or media resources officers will have very limited value, except possibly as a short-term measure. Librarians and media resources officers need to be part of the group that determines the overall selection principles, plus any anti-racist and anti-sexist working parties that are developing school policies. They can then ensure that any comprehensive document will contain within it all the measures that will support their specific initiatives with regard to resources.

Selection principles will need to take account of the following, if they are to combat negative bias in new acquisitions:

1 Are materials ordered only after prior examination and assessment?
2 Are materials checked for accuracy?
3 Has the viewpoint and attitude of the author been identified as acceptable?
4 Are materials evaluated in terms of agreed criteria? Do these include criteria for the selection of resources which are not racist, sexist or in other ways pejoratively biased?
5 Is there a conscious commitment to select resources which positively reflect ethnic minorities, women and working-class people?
6 Is there a conscious commitment to selecting stock which is accurately representative of a diversity of cultures and which reflects a global framework of knowledge?

7 Are books in the home languages of the pupils actively sought?
8 Is consultation – with colleagues and the community – part of the process of selection?
9 If materials are rejected because of blatant bias, is the publisher advised of the reason?
10 Is there a strategy to ensure that resources from specialist bookshops, local authorities and alternative publishers are considered for selection?

Selection procedures

There are few short cuts to ensuring that the new additions to the school's resources will not be pejoratively biased. Tight financial constraints mean that expensive errors simply cannot be afforded. Opportunities will have to be made to allow for materials to be thoroughly evaluated prior to purchase.

Buying a publication, or a set of textbooks, from a publisher's catalogue is tantamount to buying a domestic product because it has been appealingly advertised on the television. Yet this obviously still happens in quite a number of schools. The evidence is the proliferation and glossiness of the catalogues. Publishers spend vast sums each year on producing these glamorous and weighty advertising brochures, and more money on posting them all around the country. As publishers are not charitable organizations, it must clearly be worth their while.

Publisher's catalogues

do have a use in the school. They provide the bibliographic details such as ISBN for ordering and information on availability and price. In this respect they are more up-to-date than the standard indexes, Whitaker's Reference catalogue and British Books in Print, even when on microfiche. For re-ordering or confirming materials already evaluated, they are a convenient tool, as they are for ordering inspection copies. This latter strategy is to be recommended. As we have seen, even series that appear reliable may throw up exceptions, and even authors who have been found positive – and popular – in the past do not come with guarantees. Publishers' lists are motivated purely by commercial interest and this includes the sections to be found in some, headed 'multi-racial' or 'multi-cultural' books. Penguin's list of multicultural books for children is the one notable exception. It lists materials published by

Penguin that are deemed relevant, but it has been independently compiled by Rosemary Stones. In both her selection and her brief evaluation of each title, she provides uncompromising guidance to one section of available books.

Bibliographies

and recommended lists of reading and curriculum materials are considered to be much more trustworthy. They are often eagerly welcomed by teachers – possibly too eagerly. There is no doubt that after a full day's teaching, the task of sifting through a host of new publications is daunting in the extreme. For one thing, it cannot but be time-consuming; until time is allocated in the school term for this task, schools will not give it the attention and energy it demands. For another, many teachers doubt their own competence at judging a book effectively on brief handling; certainly this is a skill which has to be learned and enhanced through practice. Developing teachers' skills in evaluating books, needs to be a recognized component of teacher education programmes, both at initial and in-service level.

Meanwhile, teachers may continue to depend on the judgments of others. This is preferable to buying blind, but can never be wholly satisfactory. In the end, all materials are selected for a specific purpose and a particular readership; satisfactory selection is a matching process, matching the most appropriate materials available to educational objectives and a specific audience which only the purchaser can identify. All that such lists can do is to draw attention to what *is* available.

Even to provide limited guidance, such lists will have to be:

(i) *Current*: with short print runs, even the most useful books often disappear; with constant development in the debate surrounding equality in education, some materials once in favour are found wanting. With such a dearth of resources available initially, certain books had a temporary value but can now be replaced by something better.

(ii) *Informative*: since lists do not provide the materials the way that consultative collections or exhibitions do, they must at least tell prospective purchasers:
why the book is included;
who it is for, whether for class or private use;
how to obtain it: after working through this list, teachers should not have to go then to catalogues for

the necessary bibliographic details of publisher, ISBN or price. (Not all books are purchased from bookshops, which will work with information on author and title only.)

(iii) *Selective*: here as elsewhere, brevity is a virtue, confirming the essentially short span of useful life that any list of recommendations can hope to enjoy. Any attempt at comprehensiveness is only appropriate in an academic context; in the context of guidance for schools and libraries selecting new materials for a term or a year, they would be merely ponderous and intimidating. There cannot be a genuinely comprehensive list; ultimately inclusion will depend on the individual or group who has compiled it, their knowledge of the materials available, and their choices. On past record, no list of recommendations that has (whatever the compilers' intentions) been received as comprehensive, has served its audience wholly reliably. Some inclusions in non-racist lists have inevitably been attacked as actually racist. It is significant that the National Book League's first compilation of fiction; *Books for the multiracial classroom* (2nd edn 1976) contained over 350 titles; their *Wider heritage* (1980) over 200 and their latest *We all live here* is a mere 100 titles (not all of which I like!). More helpful is Bob Dixon's candidly idiosyncratic list (1982) and Judith Elkin's series (1983) in, appropriately, a periodical.

(iv) *Tentative*: it should be acknowledged by each compiler that their list is not, cannot be, authoritative. Nor should it be used uncritically. Because there are working parties or librarians who have taken on the task or identified as part of their job the scanning and evaluation of new publications that seek to combat racism and sexism, and because they have recorded their views to draw attention to potentially useful (or damaging) materials, does not mean that they set themselves up, or should be set up, as experts. They have simply done some of the groundwork, and recognize that information about it may be worth making available to others. In selecting materials for their own curriculum or their own collections, and always for their own clientele, teachers and librarians should not assume that they will be making the right purchase just because it is favourably recommended on a list compiled by X or Y.

Reviews

need to be regarded with a similar scepticism. Scanning periodicals for reviews is an excellent way of keeping informed of new publications. The reviews themselves are likely to be sufficiently detailed to be informative. As we saw in Chapter 2, more of the journals that review educational publications are becoming alerted to the issue of bias, and are likely to identify the most overt. Some reviewers, such as Beverley Anderson and Marion Glastonbury (*Times Educational Supplement*) and all those writing for *Multiracial Education*, *Multicultural Teaching*, *Spare Rib*, *Race Today*, *Race and Class*, *Issues*, *English Magazine*, or publications of such bodies as the Commission of Racial Equality are active campaigners against pejorative bias in books. In almost all professional journals, whether in the field of education, libraries or literature, the reviews are signed. It soon becomes possible to recognize which reviewers will be most helpful, but once again, they should not be the final arbiters for choice.

The same applies even to the journals that devote themselves to issues of race, sex and class in literature, particularly in children's books: *Children's Book Bulletin*, *Dragon's Teeth* and the Council for Interracial Books for Children and *Multicultural Teaching*, with its regular information service on new developments and resources for schools.

Local bulletins and lists, and those from local educational and library, groups and institutions are also valuable initial sources of new developments but, as with all reviews and lists, will have to be followed up by looking at the materials themselves. Most helpful of all are the lists (if they offer full details for ordering) that accompany and detail materials on display.

Exhibitions, displays

and bookshops, even when commercially motivated, are useful in selecting books for schools. For an overview of current publications, there is the annual London Head Teachers' Association exhibition each spring. More specialized and limited exhibitions take less time to view and can be more immediately useful: two other London-based annual events are *Books for the Third World* held at the Institute of Education in January and the *Radical Black Book Fair* in March. The Feminist Book Fair, held in June, is also impressively useful.

Even more specifically orientated to the needs of teachers are the exhibitions that are mounted to support conferences and in-service courses. The annual National Association for Multiracial Education conference, for example, offers a sales service from several ethnic minority bookshops; in other cases the display is mounted by course organizers, teachers and librarians. A commercial service is offered by Rachel Evans, who will set up and sell from a collection of current publications, from mainstream and alternative publishers and those developed locally around the country. Other similar initiatives are now operating more locally, but on similar lines. Sister-write (who will provide exhibition collections on a sale or return basis) will also save time – and potential error – in the long run. Some of these services are listed under organizations. Not only will these offer an impressive range of materials not often available elsewhere, but their staff are likely to be extremely well informed about their stock, and about the issues under scrutiny.

School books purchasing should not be wholly restricted to direct purchasing agencies, as still happens in a few regions of Britain. Selection practice in schools should allow for a certain amount of over-the-counter purchases each year. Visits to bookshops of a specialist nature, or attendance at courses with sales exhibitions, afford teachers contact with resources that is not part of their regular range of opportunity. Some of the material they note down with a view to ordering will be unobtainable by the time the order is processed. Other materials have been gathered from the Caribbean, the USA or the Indian sub-continent by the bookshops themselves. It is efficient to buy what has been examined and considered appropriate at the time that one sees it: even if there is a fair mark-up to cost in the service that has been provided, it is still likely to be cost-effective to the school. Further, our best source of anti-racist and anti-sexist materials continues to be such specialist bookshops, and they deserve as a matter of principle to be supported.

Support and guidance for selection

The most helpful guidance is to be found in specially compiled *resource collections* developed by educational and county library support services. The first of these to be established, at Inner London's Centre for Urban Educational Studies, addresses itself to issues of both race and sex, and is still open, by appointment with the librarian, to all visitors. Haringey and Brent both have impressive multicultural education resource centres, but now, fortunately, similar facilities can be found in many areas of the UK, or are in the process of being developed. Some of these are listed in the Schools

Council *Resources for multicultural education* (1984) or in full from the Multicultural Education Resource Centre at Luton. Not all these centres are open outside of school hours, but if provision for such visits is made part of the selection procedure for schools, the time will in the end have been extremely economically spent.

The established centres offer collections of materials specifically suited to combating racism and sexism in schools, and are generally concerned to keep up-to-date with new publications. They also offer expertise: their staff can identify the materials most appropriate to a specific need and discuss other possibilities. They may know how certain of the materials have been applied to maximum effect in schools and be able to suggest how best they can be used.

This kind of professional advice may also be offered by the County or Borough Library Service that supports schools or, in the case of Inner London, by the ILEA Learning Resources Branch. Expertise is provided by librarians who have familiarized themselves with the materials and are knowledgeable about the issues. Again, they can be consulted to match specific resources with curricular or leisure requirements and to offer guidance on selection and evaluation.

The aims of such services are very similar: to make their consumers (the teachers and school librarians and in some cases children's librarians in the public service) aware of bias in books and the potential consequences, and to advise on the selection of appropriate materials to support equality in education.

Other permanent consultative collections are provided by organizations. The libraries of the Commonwealth Institutes in London and Edinburgh, Waites Library of AFFOR in Birmingham and that of the Institute of Race Relations (unique in that it also carries National Front publications like *Spearhead*) may also offer a useful advisory service, but their frame of reference is in all cases far wider than schools. So are the collections of feminist literature of the Fawcett Library at the City of London Polytechnic and the Equal Opportunities Commission in Manchester.

How one school selects materials

As a final illustration of selection practices that ensure that new resources with pejorative bias are avoided, there follows my account of the principles and methods by which the librarian of a large inner city comprehensive school chooses her stock (Klein, 1983).

1   The overall responsibility – but not the sole responsibility – for selection is with the librarian – she can veto.
2   That the librarian has the final decision is totally supported by the Head.
3   Overall balance of stock is a constant concern, but not rigid in terms of every individual order.
4   The librarian asks for lists, and also of projected topics for study, from the teachers.
5   She calls for specialist advice where necessary, for example in chemistry books.
6   She asks advice also about books that worry her, using publishers' inspection systems.
7   She considers it necessary to build up basic series of information materials in all subjects.
8   She spends time on reviews in the following journals: *School Librarian* ('sometimes worrying'), the *English Magazine*, *Children's Book Bulletin*, *Multicultural Teaching*, *Dragon's Teeth*, *Radical Bookseller* and the *Times Educational Supplement*, and also consults the *Bookseller* to find out what's new, and notes items in newspapers and 'wherever I go'.
9   She sees this work as an economical use of her time, as she then has a file of 'must see' books which she takes to 'all exhibitions' and to specialist and general bookshops, so that she can go with specific purposes in mind.
10 She also goes through publishers' catalgoues to see what's new, or for ordering details, and is aware of and taps the specialist and non-standard sources.
11 She uses the loans and reference collections of CLR to see what's new, and to evaluate materials.
12 She also allows publishers to come into schools – this has the advantage that she can 'moan about what I don't like'.
13 She writes and complains to publishers about unsuitable materials, which most often means racist or sexist, and her position in the Library Association may well add weight to these complaints.
14 On the subject of racist materials also stocked, she said 'she hoped to have found them all' and would discard them if sure they were bad, or would otherwise discuss them with staff whose views she trusts. She expressed a strong wish to have access to parents in connection with evaluation, and is now suggesting that a sign is put in the library to the following effect: 'if there is something you don't like, bring it to the librarian to discuss'.

15 Mother-tongue materials are not yet stocked (this was 1981), but the librarian has already arranged to go out and buy books *with* the children who, she says, are very enthusiastic about it. She plans to consult them also on Indian stories in English.

16 On the subject of fiction, the librarian expressed strong feelings. She objected to the idea that children won't read fiction when the reality is that they are 'getting the wrong books'. Her concluding remark: 'I refuse to spend money on books (fiction) that aren't relevant to the kids'.

Tactical problems

There are two main strategic problems in providing guidance. Different organizations have resolved them in different ways:

(a) *Separate or together?*

Where should the books that will facilitate selection of materials positive on issues of sex, race and class for schools, best be displayed? They need to be part of the overall consultative collections, in their appropriate alphabetical or classified sequence on the shelves; on this there is general agreement. It was certainly found useful in the 1970s for there to be also discrete collections of books that contribute to multi-cultural education and sex equality, and many teachers would still find such collections the quickest and easiest to consult. Seeing all the materials together also makes a nice point: there is a fair amount available, and much of it is of a high standard. However useful it may be, however, to have everything in one place, it should not be achieved at the expense of the resources being lost to the general collection. Here they will at least be visible to those teachers and librarians doing a prepurchase evaluation but who still see equality in education as no particular concern of theirs.

It is important also for the books to be where the expertise is; also, for the books to travel to support courses, such as Inner London Education Authority's boxes of books for a multicultural society, one for infant, one for junior and one for nursery schools, operating from Lambeth Teachers Centre. Accordingly, many authorities recognize that more than one copy of the most effective materials will be needed.

(b) *Good and bad, or just the good?*

Certain authorities, ILEA among them, take the view that their consultative collections are there to display resources which schools may wish to buy. Books with blatant bias, when identified by one of the library staff or by a teacher, are withdrawn not only from the Loans Service, but also from the reference collection. There is a further argument that is wasteful to spend money on materials which cannot possibly be recommended.

This approach does create its own difficulties. First, there is the possibility that teachers, not knowing that a book has been withdrawn or omitted because of its bias, may buy it after seeing it elsewhere. Second, the librarians are forced to decide which books are too pejoratively biased for inclusion – and while in most cases the issue is clearcut, or the book obviously dated or dispensable, there are other examples which are controversial: *The slave dancer*, for example, or *My mate Shofiq*. A third category: 'Beans' on *Zambia* published by A and C Black, was kept on the shelves, even though there had been objections to it, because there was nothing else at that level on Zambia.

Bradford uses a different system. The full consultative collection contains the positive 'multicultural' books, but a separate collection displays the positive *and* racist books. It is housed in the office of the librarian with special responsibility for schools, so that she can 'talk to anyone who comes about them'. Such structuring of opportunity for discussion should be recognized as a major support service for selection.

Leicestershire also shelves the questionable materials in among the desirable, both in the general and in the 'multicultural' collection. Teachers coming to Thames Tower to evaluate materials will once again find a good deal of expertise among the librarians of the support service, and inside the books, they will find not one review but two. The librarians and teachers responsible for these reviews are all sensitive to bias in books: not only do they identify it in the books, but they will attempt also a qualitative judgment – again offered as the basis for discussion.

Nottingham, Newcastle and Brent are among the growing number of authorities whose library support services are concerned to combat pejorative bias in books. Whether teachers and librarians come to use the central collection and service, or whether it is in the context of the School Library Loans van's visits to schools, attention is brought to the issue of bias. It is not unusual to see a school with a rather tired library stock that is almost exclusively ethnocentric, enlivened by the presence of non-sexist materials and those which reflect cultural diversity all on loan from the library support service. It appears to be taking longer for the schools to purchase such resources for themselves, but at least the children are gaining access to some of them. ILEA also has piloted a loans service of books in community languages to schools: this again fills a gap, and it provides guidance to the school in selecting materials that the teachers cannot readily evaluate.

Additional selection guidance can be found in the *community*, and may be useful in the case of home languages, although the parent or other adult may not necessarily be concerned about issues of racial or religious bias. Students, too, can have a say in selection, but cannot be expected to work within the framework of a selection policy that aims to avoid biased materials. It is also worth reiterating that children themselves are ruthless censors. One group of teachers invited their pupils – mostly infant, a few junior – to take off the shelves of their classrooms and school library any books that they thought were biased. Off came books that were patronizing to the handicapped or to girls, every naked black child in sight, and a much loved duck called Ping, because the Chinese people in the illustrations were all coloured bright yellow. Offence was also taken to a Nipper in which the artist had used a post-Impressionist palette of blue and green to depict black characters – and a letter of protest was sent to Macmillan.

Curriculum planning

Stringent selection methods may ensure that funds are not wasted on new materials that are pejoratively biased, but the selection can only be made from what is available. Although more and better resources are coming out, it is a slow process. There may still be topics which are desirable for study but for which no relatively unbiased material exists – Livingstone's explorations would be a case in point. Curriculum development must therefore be planned in relation to resources. If the school has its own librarian, she has a clear role in such planning: otherwise professional guidance may be needed from support services. It is advisable also to seek materials from other local authorities: they may have developed and made available resources for the curricula in their own schools, such as from the Minority Group Support Service of Coventry, that would translate splendidly to other schools. Local teachers' centres and resource centres may also have information about initiatives and resources that could be adopted – or adapted. From September 1984, the Local Authorities Race Relations Information Exchange (LARRIE) has been set up to document on computer all relevant materials developed by local authorites in the UK.

Schools can also develop their own resources to support their curriculum. Again, outside support and guidance may be useful in keeping in view issues of bias. Birmingham teachers have worked at the African and Asian Resource Centre; one body of material developed there in the 1970s illustrated the early explorations of Africa in the north. It enabled the teachers to counteract the bias of all history books that not only suggest, but unequivocably state, that the Europeans 'discovered' Africa. In developing new materials for curricular areas like history and geography, guidance is available in the Development Education and the World Studies Project materials and approaches, described in Chapter 5.

Sharing information

If curriculum materials that are specifically developed prove successful in both pedagocial terms and in combating bias, a further strategy will be valuable – the sharing of the initiative. Teachers' Centres, advisers and information agents in education should be informed of the existence of such materials, so that these, or the principles behind them, can be disseminated. With a preponderance of available materials still so biased, there is no time to be wasted on inventing identical wheels all around the country, often even within the same authority. Good practice and useful materials should be shared, either through the support services of education and libraries, or through the medium of periodicals such as *Multicultural Teaching* and *Gen*.

New publications

A final set of initiatives for combating bias in materials must be acknowledged: those coming from ethnic minority publishers of the calibre of New Beacon and Bogle L'Ouverture, who have for decades been producing material that is anti-racist. Falling Wall, Black Ink and Centreprise sustain the tradition, and Virago and the Women's Press are among those providing anti-sexist materials. Inner London Education Authority's Publications Service has made a commitment to producing non-sexist and non-racist publications. Their *World in a City* bilingual materials, their *Welcome Poster, ABC frieze, Bilingual Under Fives* and *Reading through Understanding* materials are models in their field.

There is a shift, too, in the thinking of mainstream publishers. It may be that putting 'bandwagon' brown faces on covers did not sell more books; it may be that they are responding to pressure, but what matters is the outcome – the new books. These are more carefully and responsibly conceived on the whole. We who buy their products can in the long run have a good deal of influence: in order to stay in business, publishers have to sell their books. However, Bodley Head pledged itself to continue to print *Little Black Sambo* when it took over Chatto's list in 1984 'because there is still a steady demand' and in 1986 still discreetly supply it; only when schools, libraries and the informed public refuse to spend money on such racist reading matter will publishers cease churning it out.

In their pursuit of a financially restricted market, several publishers have made concerted efforts which are worth support. Collins ran its competition for fiction with a multi-ethnic theme in 1977: though two of the three of the prizewinners were white and the third, Dhondy, already in print with Macmillan, the initiative was laudable. Bodley Head and others quietly publish carefully selected and edited literature of a high standard that is free of pejorative bias. Collections like the stories of Ranjana Ash and verse edited by James Berry (Harrap), novels like Toeckey Jones's (1979) *Go well, stay well* or bilingual story books (Bodley Head) are providing positive alternatives, tossing a further gauntlet at bias.

Longman has followed the examples of McGraw Hill in the USA, and produced its own guidelines to all in-house editors. These are clear-cut and detailed, dealing with content, illustration and terminology. Such a publisher's policy promises that manuscripts with an ethnocentric or sexist approach will be turned down, and that those which are selected for publication will have any obvious lapses into pejorative bias edited out before they reach the children. A commitment by all publishers along these lines would be a guaranteed step forward, but that has not yet happened. The Educational Publishers' Council, however, has published a document on behalf of all its members (1982) stating a commitment to avoiding racist bias in new work. Anti-sexist guidelines followed in 1984. It represents an interesting volte-face: only two years earlier, a panel of practitioners in multicultural education was strongly resisted by the members of the EPC who had invited them to give a seminar. The old arguments then were predictable: authors are creative; it is not our role to inhibit them because someone may not like what they say, and: our market is shrinking so drastically, we're so desperately threatened that we can't start taking on these (new!) issues now. It was pointed out, and may have come to their attention frequently in the following two years, that it was their old and biased books that were no longer selling too well; at any event, they have officially now adopted the opposite stance. Results can be awaited with interest and a modicum of hope.

Macmillan holds in-house seminars of a similar nature, but so far there is no (public) in-house statement of policy regarding bias. They have also linked with Save the Children to publish David Moore's booklet in 1979 *Multicultural Britain: a personal view* in 1980 and the *Patterns of Living* (1981) series described in Chapter 6.

Other publishers, Penguin, Hodder, Heinemann Children's Books, OUP, Ginn and Ward Lock among them, are in frequent consultation over issues of bias in manuscripts. They seek the advice, of practitioners in multicultural education or gender equality, of members of ethnic communities, of feminists, of teachers and librarians. This increased sensitivity and sense of responsibility on the part of those publishers that provide, still, the bulk of resources encountered by children, also gives grounds for optimism.

Some of their number are even prepared to take financial risks. Methuen's *Terraced House Readers* were so enthusiastically received for their non-racist, non-sexist and classless approach, as well as their intrinsic merit, that teachers' centres, notably Bedford's English Language Resource Centre, pressured them into producing a poster that would further support language development for young children. The printing of 100 copies of a colour poster left Methuen out of pocket, but the response by practitioners was so enthusiastic that they nevertheless followed it with a set of four colour posters. Then came new pressure, this time notably from the Centre for Urban Educational Studies, that other language versions of the *Terraced House Readers* be made available. In complying, Methuen found themselves in a quagmire of linguistic problems: no two translators agreed on one version of Bengali, and endless modifications were made, but the printed version was still found to be inaccurate – so Methuen withdrew it, and began again. Now a new version of Bengali, plus one in Urdu which also takes account of subtle differences in culture (e.g. 'changing my clothes' is preferable to 'taking off my clothes') are available, to be followed by Turkish and then other community languages. They have been produced in an ingenious form of adhesive strips, which can be stuck on alongside – or, better still, directly over – the English on each page.

Other publishers taking risks are those for whom social issues, racism, sexism and class bias among them, determine the nature of all their publications in a way that may easily diminish their returns. Writers and Readers and Pluto Press are two such houses and their publications like those of, say, the Women's Press, individually and collectively challenge bias in books. Smaller presses are springing up around the UK with a similar commitment; one called Arawidi is devoted to children's books validating a range of dialects of English. All of this led Rosemary Stones (1982) to observe that:

> the emergence of a wider and more socially aware audience for children's books has gone hand-in-hand with the beginnings of regular and progressive reviewing. Mainstream yardsticks are no longer the only ones available. There are now progressive alternatives.

Conclusions

The concept of censorship is sometimes used to attack or even prevent the considerations of bias in selecting new books for school or library collections. It is important that the emotions should not be so stirred that debate and discussion of the issues are inhibited. It is impossible to buy all the books that are published for children, and in seeking only the best we should automatically be discarding those most pejoratively biased.

In order to select wisely, however, materials need to be examined and evaluated prior to purchase. This is time-consuming, but the only way to ensure that money is spent on the best and most appropriate materials. Reviews and lists cannot be wholly relied on and publishers' catalogues are no guide to the merit of the books featured. The best form of guidance are the specialist resource collections, where there will be advisers who are sufficiently familiar with their stock to be able to recommend the most appropriate books to prospective purchasers. Visits to exhibitions and ethnic minority bookshops are also cost-effective in the long run, especially if one can buy on sight. Support and guidance on selection are also part of the library support services to schools, and in many cases there are particular facilities to inform on appropriate – and inappropriate – materials for a multicultural society. There may be other local agencies which specialize in developing new materials specifically designed to extend the school curriculum towards multicultural education. Certain publishers, both mainstream and 'alternative' are continuing to fill the many gaps in resources and are seeking, through more consultation and also heightened sensitivity in house, to produce genuinely useful books. What is still to be adequately developed in the UK is an efficient system of disseminating information about these new developments; at present the task is taken on piecemeal by numerous organizations and several periodicals, with varying effectiveness.

Overall, however, there are now forces combating the perpetuation of racism in publications, just as there are classroom strategies and school policies that can tackle bias in existing stock. As yet a tiny army, but with the support of practitioners who select the books that will be put into the hands of tomorrow's adults, the battle may still be won. For in the end, we should be aiming for a degree of awareness and confidence on the part of readers that would allow them to deal with any publication, however biased. Yet the battle should be fought also for more accurate, appropriate publications which seek to serve the interests not of the dominant group but of the readers themselves.

Chapter 10

Conclusions: The watershed

This review of the issue of bias in children's materials has shown that, while books continue to be the prime learning resource for children and adults and continue to have a following for private leisure, the bulk of them are perniciously biased. Pejorative bias is far-reaching in its effects and occurs in all areas of children's literature and learning resources.

Increasingly, educational practitioners are acknowledging these realities and taking action to combat the potentially damaging effects of bias in materials. They are discussing the issues, developing their own awareness and sensitivity and their own skills in appraising materials. They are developing approaches to combating the effects of biased books in the schools and teaching children to challenge the authority of the printed word and to trust in their own judgment. When selecting new resources, bias is more frequently a criterion for rejection.

Practitioners are extending the school curriculum in relation to available positive resources, and into areas that will give students a wider understanding of people of other races, other cultures, other classes and the opposite sex. They are designing a school curriculum founded on a global, rather than an ethnocentric perspective, and creating an ethos in the school that allows for discussion of issues of racism and sexism.

Practitioners are responding to Local Education Authority policy documents on issues of equality in education, and developing similar policies for their individual schools. They are alert to the statements and recommendations of government, national and professional bodies which declare prejudice, inequality and discrimination to be abhorrent in our society. Views like 'I treat them all the same' or 'Now they're here, they should become like us' are no longer officially acceptable, although they will always have a following.

Alternative publishers and teachers themselves have created a small body of positive materials and several that actively challenge derogatory bias. Mainstream publishers are recognizing increasingly that biased books are a commercial risk and are seeking to avoid producing them. Some have even shown a sincere commitment to publishing materials to meet the cultural and linguistic needs of Britain's ethnic minorities. Support services in the form of organizations, LEA advisers, information agents and specific periodicals disseminate information about these new developments. Sexism is neither so easily dismissed as the preoccupation of feminists, nor multicultural education as the treatment of black schoolchildren.

Here, then, is the watershed. A good many purveyors and producers of books and materials have yet to reach it, however. In society at large, the reality of racism is often denied by white people, and feminism may still be ridiculed. Newspapers, TV and much of the literature perpetuate such views. Many whites are resisting the possibility of change – change is uncomfortable and may appear threatening to their dominant position. The media offer reassurance that the campaign for greater social equality is marshalled by a few 'extremists' or is the province of one small political group – or that it is all a trend that will pass or just a joke.

There are educational practitioners who still regard social issues as interfering with and undermining the school curriculum, taking time from the three R's or the examination syllabuses. Multicultural education, one teacher commented to me during her summer holiday is 'very in', clearly hoping that it would soon be 'out'. She still perceived it as something extra, a chore that would demand additional time in school and would impinge on what she was trying to do – which was, she no doubt believed, her best. To her, multicultural education appears threatening; to many it still appears irrelevant. Countermanding the articulate attacks that diminish multicultural education as 'samosas and saris' makes the task of demonstrating its relevance to *all* of tomorrow's citizens harder still.

Those who resist the need for change in society and in education also consider that children's books are fine as they are. They counterattack the campaigners with cries of 'oversensitive' and hold our rich heritage of children's literature sacrosant. Policy directives from their education authority or professional bodies will be met with resistance, but they are one way to impel practitioners to recognize the issues. Even more effective will be the creation of a social climate in which prejudice and discrimination are regarded as abhorrent; where the dominant can be made to see that, to a lesser degree than the dominated, they are nevertheless also losers in a divisive society.

The subtle and partial change in social climate is encapsulated by a review of the Children's Book Awards of 1983 by Mary Hoffman (*Times Educational Supplement*, September 1983). She points out that Roald Dahl's *The BFG* would have been the fourth book on the Carnegie shortlist 'if some panellists hadn't found its national stereotype jokes – such as Greeks being greasy – unacceptable. You can bet that wouldn't have happened ten years ago!' No one bets against certainties, but the fact remains that *The BFG did* win the Children's Book Award given by the Federation of Children's Book Groups.

So the campaign needs to continue. Some of the ways forward are now summarized:

1 Societal pressure for change

Racism is being acknowledged as a white problem; black people suffer the effects of the problem. Some white people are working at confronting their racism. Support is available through racism awareness programmes, some of which are oriented towards people working in education. Other changes, though small and slow, are becoming apparent. Racism is no longer considered to be acceptable nor discrimination desirable – justifications have to be sought. The women's movement is reaching further into society. Self-help and community groups are mushrooming around the UK, many of them challenging racism, sexism and prejudice in society. The climate is subtly changing.

2 Policies and recommendations

The DES has publicly acknowledged an educational obligation to all children in relation to our multicultural society. LEAs have published their own policy statements on equality of education – nearly thirty to date. Teachers hitherto isolated in their attempts to combat racism and sexism in their school may now find that they are supported by a document issued by their LEA. Such statements have a potential for supporting and initiating change in the short-term. Most draw specific attention to the presence of bias in books and its potential for harm.

Certain authorities, notably the ILEA, having provided a detailed framework of policy and approach, have thrown the onus back on the schools. Schools are being asked to formulate their own anti-racist and anti-sexist policies. Supported by extra funding, they are being invited to examine their objectives, practice, curriculum, and not least, resources, in terms of equality of education.

Professional bodies, including the NUT, AMMA and the Library Association have also issued declarations against racism and sexism in professional practice. Supportive guidelines and advice have also been provided, and such bodies are working collaboratively with agencies such as the CRE and EOC.

3 In-service and initial training

The position has not radically changed since John Eggleston and his team produced their report for the DES (1981). They found that courses on in-service Teacher Education were, in a multi-racial society, insufficient, often inadequate in content and sporadic, and that they may not be locally available. Nor is take-up what it should be. Nevertheless, initiatives are in evidence, and provision in terms of both quantity and quality is improving. As a result of authoritative pressure, it can be expected that more practitioners will recognize the relevance of such courses to enhancing their professional competence.

Initial training was reviewed by Giles and Cherington in a paper in Craft (1981). They identified that most multicultural education was offered in the form of an option. Until it is an intrinsic part of the overall training, consideration of issues of educational equality will not be part of the thinking of our future teachers.

There is some evidence that initial training organizations are recognizing this reality; something may be done about it. New initiatives have recently been developed at both initial and in-service level – two are described by Crispin Jones and Rosalind Street-Porter (1983).

The DES has also set up six urban regional centres for training the trainers; a national programme of short courses on Teacher Education in a Multicultural Society. It is hoped that these initial courses will generate course outlines and other resource materials for teacher trainers. Once again, the courses draw attention to the curriculum materials used in schools, and opportunities are created to keep trainers informed about new publications for teachers that will develop their knowledge and understanding about issues of educational equality. These centres could also, if properly staffed and resourced, disseminate information about new developments in the field. (Details in *Multicultural Teaching* 2.1 or from Education Department, Nottingham University.)

4 School-based initiatives

are taking place, sometimes with the support of additional funding and outside advice. A powerful structure for change is built in a school that is working as a whole to re-evaluate its educational objectives and practice in terms of educational equality. Inevitably curriculum and resources will come under review, and agreements will have to be reached over the issue of bias in resources.

As part of a re-evaluation of professional practice, attention may be given to the teachers' role in helping children to learn for themselves. There is a valuable way forward if teachers and school librarians acknowledge that part of this task must be actively to teach their students to challenge everything they read, seek alternative sources, and develop and ultimately trust their own judgment.

5 Developing new materials

As teachers extend the curriculum and accordingly develop new resources, they have the opportunity to challenge traditional biases. They can seek to build into the new resources an approach that demands individual thought, rather than unquestioning acceptance, from their pupils. They can, too, design materials along a model (described as diagram 4 in Chapter 5) which overtly challenges ethnocentricism and sexism.

Teachers and librarians have, through their spending budgets, the power to influence commercial publishers. Three main strategies have been found effective:

(i) Protest and boycott of pejoratively biased materials. Letters of protest are taken seriously by publishers, and advantage can also be taken of informal opportunities afforded by, for example, the London Head Teachers' Association Exhibition (see p. 129) where it is often commissioning editors and senior sales representatives who are servicing the stand.

(ii) Positive praise or pressure: publishers have acceded to requests to develop materials along certain lines, or have actively sought manuscripts that will meet needs expressed by members of their market. Further effectiveness may be achieved by expressions of praise to publishers for new materials that are anti-racist and anti-sexist, and not just those of complaint.

(iii) Collaboration and consultation: this is mainly initiated by publishers, who approach educational practitioners for advice. Such contacts should be fostered as another potential avenue for progress on issues of bias in new work.

One recent strategy which appeared extraordinarily effective and was certainly quite new, took place in 1982 at London Institute of Education's University Centre for Teachers, initiated by the Librarian, Dr Norman Beswick. A course of six lectures on *Books, Libraries and Resources for a Multicultural Society* included one contribution by a commissioning editor of a large educational publishing house. She kept her talk brief and took full advantage of one-and-a-half hours of discussion to explore the views and requirements of some of the sixty or so teachers and librarians attending the course.

(iv) Supporting alternative publishers and ethnic minority, women's and other specialist bookshops and exhibition services will facilitate the availability of more positive materials.

6 Redressing the balance

At no stage have campaigners against racism, sexism and class bias in books suggested that our entire vast heritage of children's literature be discarded. That awesome body of books, however, asserts overall that only white people exist, only the middle class matter, and that boys will be boys and girls will be good.

There is a steadily growing body of books that says otherwise. Fiction that tells a good story and tells it well, featuring girls with minds of their own and positive characters from ethnic minorities; reflecting the culturally diverse nature of our cities and towns. There are new classroom materials that unselfconsciously acknowledge in their text and illustrations that not all British school children are of one class, race, colour or sex, nor do they all speak the same language or observe the same customs and religion. There are curriculum materials which have avoided the ethnocentric approach, have sought and even achieved a global perspective. There are resources that inform about cultures that now enrich Britain; that express a range of views about the world.

There are also the publications and information agencies that disseminate information about such materials. It is no longer difficult for a teacher or librarian to ascertain what is available and from where. There are opportunities for examining such materials, and there is support in the form of professional expertise about them.

One or ten such positive materials will not transform a stock cupboard, still less a library, but a collection built on the principle of giving a range of views and covering areas of knowledge that go far beyond the ethnocentric is not impossible, even with the resources available at present.

If the children in our schools have had their own evaluative skills developed and encounter resources which demonstrate that there is more than one way of viewing the world, and that all are equally valid, then something can be done to mitigate the bias in books and resources. But the racism that is embedded in the structure of our society will have to be eradicated before we can expect the publications of that society to be no longer racist.

Bibliography

Chapter 1

Alcott, L.M. *Little Women*, Puffin edn (1983).

Armstrong, W. (1973) *Sounder*, Puffin.

Banfield, B. (1980) in Preiswerk, R. (ed.), *The Slant of the pen; racism in children's books*, World Council of Churches.

Bayfield, T. (1980) *Churban; the murder of the Jews of Europe* London, Michael Goulston Foundation.

Bernheim, M. (1974) *In Africa*, Lutterworth.

Coolidge, S. *What Katy did*, Collins edn, (1967).

Fisher, S. and Hicks, D. (1985) *World Studies 8–13*, Oliver and Boyd.

Fitzhugh, L. (1976) *Nobody's family is going to change*, Gollancz.

Glastonbury, M. (1982) 'What books tell girls' *English magazine*, no. 9.

Le Guin, U. (1971) *Wizard of Earthsea*, Penguin.

Guy, R. (1974) *Edith Jackson*, Gollancz.

Lee, H. (1960) *To Kill a Mockingbird*, Pan edn (1974).

de la Mare, W. (1977) *Collected stories for children*, Puffin.

Montgomery, L.M. *Anne of Green Gables*, Puffin edn (1977).

Reading On. Red Book One. Oliver and Boyd 1958, 11th impression 1975.

Schools Council (1981) *Education for a multiracial society: Curriculum and context 5–13*, Longmans Resources Unit.

Sivanandan, A. (1982) *A different hunger*, Pluto Press.

Taylor, T. (1973) *The Cay*, Puffin.

Worrall, M. (1978) 'Multiracial Britain and the Third World: tensions and approaches in the classroom *New Era*, vol. 59, no. 2.

Chapter 2

Afro-Caribbean Education Research Project (1981) *Education and the Afro-Caribbean child*, ACER (see organisations).

Adams, C. (1982) *Ordinary lives; a hundred years ago*, Virago.

Adams, C. and Laurikietis, R. (1976) *The gender trap: a closer look at sex roles* bk 3 *Messages and images*, Quartet.

Ajegbo, K. (1983) 'Black life in a white world' in *Teaching London Kids*, no. 19.

Alexander, Z. (1982) *Library services and Afro-Caribbean Communities*, Association of Assistant Librarians.

Bannerman, H. (1874) *Little Black Sambo*, Bodley (1984).

Bettelheim, B. (1976) *The uses of enchantment; the meaning and importance of fairy tales*, Penguin.

Brandreth, G. (1979) *Here comes Golly*, Pelham.

Buckingham, D. (1983) 'Positive images?' *Multicultural Teaching*, vol. 2 no. 1.

Burgess, C. (1980) 'Breakthrough to sexism'. *Teaching London Kids*, no. 12.

Coard, B. (1974) *How the West Indian child is made educationally subnormal in the British School system*, New Beacon.

Colbert, J.H. (1960) *Children of the Cape*, Hutchinson.

Commission for Racial Equality (1973) *Checklist against racism and sexism*, CRE.

Dixon, B. (1976) *Catching them young*, Pluto Press.

Elkin, J. (1983) 'Multicultural books' *Books for Keeps* (through 6 issues, 1983).

Goodall, P. (1982) 'Children's books: a feminist view' in *Schooling and culture* vol. 10, June 1982.

Gundara, Jagdish (1983) 'The school in multicultural society' *Multicultural Teaching*, vol. 2, no. 1.

Gundara, Jaswinder and Warwick, R. (1981) 'Myth or reality?', *Assistant Librarian*, vol. 74, no. 5.

Hicks, D. (1980) *Minorities*, Heinemann Educational.

Hill, J. *et al.* (1971) *Books for children*, Institute of Race Relations.

Hill, J. (1973) *Children are people*, Hamilton.

Home Affairs Committe (1981) *Racial disadvantage* HMSO.

Inner London Education Authority (1978) *Assessing children's books in a multiethnic society*, ILEA and CUES.

Inner London Education Authority (1980) *Education for a multiethnic society; an aide memoire for the Inspectorate*, ILEA Publications.

Klein, G. (1982) *Resources for multicultural education, an introduction*, 2nd revised edn. 1984, York. Longmans Resource Unit for Schools Council.

Lurie, A. (1980) *Clever Gretchen and other forgotten folk tales*, Heinemann.

Mackay, D. *et al.* (1970) *Breakthrough to literacy*, Longman.

Meek, M. (ed.) (1978) *The cool web*, Bodley Head.

Milner, D. (1975) *Children and race*, Penguin.

Milner, D. (1983) *Children and race 10 years on*, Ward Lock.

Perkins, T. (1979) 'Rethinking Stereotypes', in M. Barrett, (ed.) *Ideology and cultural production*, Croom Helm.

Bibliography

Spender, D. (1980) *Man made language*, Routledge & Kegan Paul.
Stanley, (ed.) (1980) *The end*, Puffin.
Stones, R. (1980) 'Radically revised reading schemes?' in *Children's Book Bulletin* no. 3.
Tucker, N. (1981) *The child and the book; psychological and literary exploration*, Cambridge.
Whitehead, F. *et al.* (1977) *Children and their books*, MacMillan.

Chapter 3

Adams, C. (1982) *Ordinary lives: a hundred years ago*, Virago.
Adams, C. and Laurikietis, R. (1976) *The gender trap: a closer look at sex roles* bk 3 *Messages and images*, Quartet.
Brandreth, G. (1979) *Here comes Golly*, Pelham.
Buckingham, D. (1983) 'Positive images?' *Multicultural Teaching* vol. 2, no. 1.
Burgess, C. (1980) 'Breakthrough to sexism' *Teaching London Kids*, no. 12.
Colbert, J.H. (1960) *Children of the Cape*, Hutchinson.
Dixon, B. (1977) *Catching them Young*, Pluto Press.
Lurie, A. (1980) *Clever Gretchen and other forgotten folktales*, Heinemann.
Mackey, D. *et al.* (1970) *Breakthrough to literacy*, Longman.
Milner, D. (1975) *Children and race*, Penguin.
Perkins, T. (1979) 'Rethinking stereotypes' in M. Barratt (ed.), *Ideology and Cultural production*, Croom Helm.
Stanley, (*ed.*) (1980) *The end*, Puffin.
Stones, R. (1980) 'Radically revised reading schemes?' in *Children's Book Bulletin*, no. 3.
Young, E. (1978) *Terrible Nung Gwama*, Collins.

Chapter 4

Ashley, B. (1976) *Trouble with Donovan Croft*, Oxford University Press.
Ashley, B. (1978) *Kind of wild justice*, Oxford University Press.
Beauty and the Beast, (1976), Dragon's World.
Beier, Ulli, (1982) *Yoruba*, Cambridge University Press.,
Bishop, C. (1936) *The five Chinese brothers*, Bodley Head.
Cox, J. (1979) *The A-Z of Man*, Nelson Dorcan Scheme.
Dhondy, F. (1976) *East End at your feet*, MacMillan.
Dickinson, P. (1972) *The Devil's children*, Penguin.
Dickinson, P. (1979) *Tulku*, Gollancz.
Explore-a-story, (1979) ILEA and Collins.
Garfield, L. (1973) *Lucifer Wilkins*, Heinemann.
Glastonbury, M. (1980) 'Patriarchal attitudes, the classics', *New Statesman*, November 1980.

Interracial Books for Children vol. 15 nos. 2 and 4, 1984 from CIBC, 1841, Broadway, New York, NY.

Kaye, G. (1980) *Beautiful Chinese Take-away Palace*, Kaye & Ward.

Lashley, J. (1972) 'Can comics join the multiracial society?' *Times Educational Supplement*, 24 September 1972.

Le Guin, U. (1968) *Wizard of Earthsea*, Penguin (1977).

Lurie, A. (1980) *Clever Gretchen and other forgotten folktales*, Heinemann.

de la Mare, W. (1977) *Collected stories for children*, Puffin.

Mitchell, M. (1936) *Gone with the wind*, MacMillan.

Needle, J. (1978) *My mate Shofiq*, Deutsch.

Preiswerk, R. (ed.) (1980) *Slant of the pen*, WCC.

Price, W. *African adventure*, Cape (1963, reissued 1971).

Resch, B. (1977) *Singing bird*, Black.

Rosenberg, S. (1976) *Will there never be a prince?* MacMillan.

Rosten, L. (1982) *Horray for Yiddish*, Elm Tree Books.

Share-a-story, (1977) ILEA and Holmes McDougall.

Steel, F.A. (1884) *Tales from the Punjab*, Bodley Head (1984).

Stones, R. (1983) *Pour out the cocoa, Janet: Sexism in children's books*. York, Longmans Resource Unit for Schools Council.

Tate, J. (1980) *Ben and Annie*, Cassells.

Twain, M. *Huckleberry Finn* Puffin edn 1983.

Wallace, J. (1982) in *Washington Post*, 4 November 1982.

Williams, J. (1979) *The Practical Princess and other liberating fairy tales*, Chatto & Windus.

Williams, U. (1980) *The Nine lives of island MacKenzie*, Carousel.

Chapter 5

Augier, F.R. and Gordon, S.C. (1962) *Sources of West Indian history*, Longman.

BEANS Series 1981 A & C Black e.g. *Mexico*.

Bennett, O. (1982) *Patterns of living*, MacMillan.

Ceserani, G.P. (1979) *Travels of Livingstone*, Kestrel.

Claire, H. (1983) *Patterns of living* reviewed in *Multicultural Teaching* 1.2.

Crawford, S. (1970) *Man alone*, Longman.

Curtis, A. (1969) *Oxford Junior book on Africa*, Oxford University Press.

Davies, A. (1970) *Problems around us*, Holmes MacDougall.

Davidson, B. (1966) *Black mother*, Penguin.

Davidson, B. (1968) *African Kingdom*, Time-Life.

Explorers (1973) MacDonald Education.

Explorers (1981) MacMillan Colour Library.

File, N. and Power, C. (1980) *Black settlers in Britain 1555–1958*, Heinemann Educational.

Fisher, S. and Hicks, D. (1985) *World Studies 8–13*, Oliver & Boyd.

Bibliography

Gill, D. (1983) 'Geography, society and the multicultural school' *Multicultural Teaching* vol. 1, no. 2.

Harries, A. (1980) *Sound of the Gora*, Heinemann.

'How they live now' series (1980) Lutterworth e.g. *Ravi of India*.

Hum Gar Chan (1980) *Ancient Chinese* reviewed in *Children's Book Bulletin* no. 5.

Inner London Education Authority (1980) *Assessing children's books for a multi-ethnic society*, (ILEA).

Lai Po Kan (1980) *Ancient Chinese*, MacDonald Educational.

McIver, A. (1939, 1978) *First Aid in English*, R. Gibson.

Mitter, S. (1980) *Living in Calcutta*, Wayland.

Preiswerk, R. (ed.) (1980) *Slant of the pen*, (WCC).

Richardson, R. (1976) *Fighting for freedom*, Nelson.

Seacole, M. (1984) *Wonderful adventures in many lands*, Falling Wall Press.

Shyllon, F. (1974) *Black slaves in Britain*, Oxford University Press.

Shyllon, F. (1977) *Black people in Britain 1555–1833*, Oxford University Press.

Thewlis, J. (1980) 'Worlds apart' *Children's Book Bulletin* no. 4.

World Studies Project (1979) *Seeing and perceiving; films in a world of change*, CWDE.

World Studies Project (1980) *Ideas into action; curriculum for a changing world*, CWDE.

Zeiris, J. (1975) *Race, science and society*, Allen & Unwin.

Chapter 6

Ahlberg, A. (1974) *Here are the Brick Street Boys*, Collins.

Ahlberg, A. (1980) *Mr Cosmo the Conjuror*, Penguin.

Bahree, P. (1982) *The Hindu World*, MacDonald.

Bruce, R. and Wallbank, J. (1982) *Beginning Religion*. Edward Arnold.

Butler, R. (1982) *Life among the Sikhs* in Friends and Neighbours series, Edward Arnold.

Carr, F. (1981) *A second book of 101 assembly stories*, Foulsham.

Craft, A. & Bardell, G. (eds) (1984) *Curriculum opportunities in a multicultural society*, Harper and Row.

Dhondy, F. (1983) 'The appropriate slant', *Times Educational Supplement* 8 July 1983.

Encyclopaedia of music (1979), Ward Lock.

Fletcher, H. *et al.* (1979) *Mathematics for Schools*, Addison Wesley.

Floyd, L. (1980) *Indian musical instruments*, Oxford.

Gatland, K. and Jefferis, D. (1982) *The world of the future*, Usbourne.

Gilroy, B. (1973) *New People at 24, Vistor from home*, Nipper series, MacMillan.

Gombrich, E.H. (1972) *Story of art*, (12th edn), Phaidon.

Groves, P. (1974) *Bangers and Mash*, Longman.

Groves, P. (1975) *Red Indians and red spots*, Longman.

Heapy, R. and Garside (1978) *Merrywhang*, Oxford.

Hemmings, R. (1983) *Assessment at 16+; Mathematics* Longmans Resources Unit for Schools Council.

Hemmings, R. (1984) 'Mathematics in Craft, A. and Bardell, G. (eds) *Curriculum opportuntiies in a multicultural society.*

Janson, H.W. (1982) *History of art for young people*, (2nd edn), Thames and Hudson.

Hynds, M. (1976) *Mumbo Jumbo*, Blackie (Sparks).

Knight, C. (1983) 'The Evaluation of reading schemes for use in the multicultural classroom' *Multicultural Teaching*, vol. 2 no. 1.

Kendall (1972) *The World of Musical Instruments*, Hamlyn.

O & B Maths Bank II (1979), Oliver and Boyd.

Oxford junior companion to music (1979), Oxford.

Perambulavil, V. (1983) 'Children's Libraries in a multi-ethnic city state', *Multicultural Teaching* vol. 2 no. 1.

Preiswerk, R. (ed.) (1980) *The Slant of the Pen*, World Council of Churches.

Ross, A. (1984) *The story of mathematics*, A & C Black.

Ruddell, D. (1982) *Recognising racism*, Birmingham Education Department. (Film strip or tape/slide).

Scholes, P. (1970) *Oxford companion to music*, (10th edn), Oxford.

Scope (1971) Longman.

Shepherd, F. (1982) 'Music in multicultural teaching', *Multicultural Teaching* vol. 1 no. 2.

Tate, J. (1976) *Crow and the brown boy* (Anchor Series), Cassell.

Thame, R. (1982) *World of Islam*, MacDonald.

Zaslavsky, C. (1979) *Africa Counts; numbers and patterns in African culture*, New York, Lawrence Hill.

Zaslavsky, C. (1980) *Count on your fingers African style*, New York, Thomas Y. Crowell.

Zaslavsky, C. (1982) *Tic Tac Toe and other three-in-a-row games from Ancient Egypt to the modern computer*, New York, Thomas Y. Crowell.

Chapter 7

Agard, J. (1983) *Limbo dancer in dark glasses*, Greenheart.

Bayfield, T. (1980) *Churban, the murder of the Jews of Europe*, Michael Goulston Foundation.

Berry, J. (1981) *Bluefoot Traveller*, Harrap.

Bullock Report (1975) *Language for life*, HMSO.

Carrington, B. and Wood, E. (1982) 'Body talk: images of sport in a multiracial school', *Multiracial Education* vol. 1 no. 2.

Dhondy, F. (ed.) (1980) *Black explosion in British Schools*, Race Today Collective.

Edwards, V. (1983) *Language in Multicultural Classrooms*, Batsford.

Bibliography

Eggleston, S.J. (1984) *Multicultural teaching: the qualitative aspects*. Paper presented to The Hague Club.

Eggleston, J. (1977) *The sociology of the school curriculum*, Routledge & Kegan Paul.

File, N. and Power, C. (1980) *Black Settlers in Britain 1555–1958*, Heinemann Educational.

Fisher, H.A.L. (1969) *History of Europe*, Fontana.

Foster, M. (1983) Review of M. Saunders; *Multicultural Teaching* (Batsford 1982) in *Multicultural Teaching* vol. 1. no. 2.

Garvie, E. (1983) The multicultural hinterland. *Multicultural Teaching* vol. 1, no. 2.

Gilbert, M.C. (1975) *Atlas of the Holocaust*, Michael Joseph.

Gill, D. (1983) 'Geography, society and the multicultural school', *Multicultural Teaching* vol. 1 no. 2.

Hemmings, R. (1984) in Craft, A. and Bardell, G. (eds). *Curriculum opportunities in a multicultural society*, Harper and Row.

Huntley, A. (1977) *At School Today*, Bogle O'Ouverture.

Inner London Education Authority (1976) *Share-a-story*, ILEA Publications.

Inner London Education Authority (1977) *Explore-a-story*, ILEA Publications, (both Reading Through Understanding Project).

Inner London Education Authority, English Centre, *Our Lives* (1978) *English Magazine*, *The Language Book* (1981) *City Lines* (1983).

Inner London Education Authority (1982) *Caribbean Authology*, ILEA Publications.

Johnson, L.K. (1975) *Dread, beat and blood*, Bogle L'Ouverture.

Milner, D. (1983) *Children and race; 10 years on*, Ward Lock Educational.

Preiswerk, R. (ed.) (1980) *The slant of the pen*, World Council of Churches.

Reading Through Understanding (1976) Project at Inner London Education Authority, Centre for Urban Educational Studies (see bibliography in Teacher's Notes for *Share-a-story*).

Rhue, M. (1982) *The Wave*, Kestrel, Penguin.

Rosen, H. and Burgess, T. (1980) *Languages and dialects of London school children*, Ward Lock.

Seacole, M. (1984) *Wonderful adventures of Mary Seacole in many lands*, Falling Wall Press.

Stone M. (1981) *The Education of the black child in Britain: the myth of multiracial education*, Collins Fontana.

Stones, R. (1983) *Pour out the cocoa, Janet: Sexism in children's books*, York, Longmans Resource Unit for School Council.

Studies in Design Education Craft and Technology 1983 vol. 15 no. 1.

Trudgill, P. (1974) *Sociolinguistics; an introduction*, Penguin.

Chapter 8

Beswick, N. (1977) *Resource based learning*, Heinemann Educational.

154

Bethell, A. (1981) *Viewpoint*, Cambridge University Press.

Blyton, E. 'Story of the little black doll' in *Stories at bedtime*, Chatto 1968.

Brandreth, G. (1979) *Here comes Golly*, Pelham.

Buckingham, D. (1984) 'Positive images?' *Multicultural Teaching* vol. 2, no. 1.

Bullock, A. (1975) *Language for life*, HMSO.

CASSOE Newsletter, 7 Pickwick Court, London, SE9.

Dahl, R. (1964) *Charlie and the chocolate factory*, Penguin.

Dhondy, F. 'Appropriate slant' *Times Educational Supplement* 8 July 1983.

Fawcett Library *Bbiliofem*, London.

Hicks, D. (1981) *Bias in geography texts*, Centre for Multicultural Education, London Institute of Education.

Home Affairs Committee (1981) *Racial disdavantage*, HMSO.

Inner London Education Authority (1976) Hey, butterfly.

Inner London Education Authority, English Centre (1978) *Our lives*.

Inner London Education Authority, English Centre (1983) *City Lines*.

Larrabeti, M. de (1981) *The Borribles go for broke*, Bodley Head.

Multicultural Education Abstracts (three issues per annum), Carfax Publishing.

National Union of Teachers (1979) *In black and white*.

Rampton, A. *Interim report* (1981) *West Indian children in our schools*, HMSO.

Scarman, (1981) *The Brixton disorders . . . inquiry report*, HMSO.

Searle, C. (1977) *World in a classroom*, Writers and Readers.

Stenhouse, L. (1982) *Teaching about Race Relations: Problems and Effects*, Routledge & Kegan Paul.

Chapter 9

Ash, R. (1980) *Short stories from India, Pakistan and Bangladesh*, Harrap.

Ballin, R. *et al.* (eds) (1980) *Wider heritage*, National Book League.

Bannerman (1884) *Little Black Sambo*, Chatto.

Bennett, O. (1982) *Patterns of living*, MacMillan.

Berry, J. (ed.) (1981) *Bluefoot Traveller*, Harrap.

Dhondy, F. (1976) *East End at your feet*, MacMillan.

Dixon, B. (1982) *Now read on*, Pluto.

Educational Publishers Council (1982) *Publishing for a multicultural society*, EPC.

Elkin, J. (1971) *Multiracial books for the classroom*, Youth Libraries Group and National Book League.

Elkin, J. (1983) 'Lifeline 2: Multicultural Books, *Books for Keeps* (six issues, through 1983).

Fox, P. (1979) *The slave dancer*, MacMillan Educational.

Gen. Women's Education Group ILEA Drama and Tape Centre, Princeton Street, London WC1.

Bibliography

Goodall, P. (1982) 'Children's books: a feminist view' in *Schooling and Culture* no 10.

Heaslip. P. (1978) *Terraced House readers*, Methuen.

Inner London Education Authority *BUF Videocassettes and Guide*.

Inner London Education Authority *Reading Through Understanding*.

Inner London Education Authority *Face Play*.

Inner London Education Authority *Welcome Poster*.

Inner London Education Authority *ABC Frieze* (Full catalogue from CLR, 275 Kennington Lane, London SE11).

Jones, T. (1979) *Go well, stay well*, Bodley Head.

Kesterton, A. (1983) *We all live here*, National Book League.

Klein. G. (1983) *The School Library and multicultural awareness*, Trentham Books and *Educational Libraries Bulletin*, University of London Institute of Education.

Multicultural Teaching, Trentham Books, 30 Wenger Crescent, Trentham, Staffs.

Needle, J. (1979) *My mate Shofiq* (Lions).

Petersen, P. (1979) *Zambia*, A & C Black.

Shawcroft, C. (1983) 'Sense or censorship', *Multicultural Teaching*, vol. 2. no 1.

Stones, R. (compiler) (1982) *Penguin Multi-Ethnic Booklist*, Penguin.

Wright, J.A. (1977, 82) *Bilingualism in education*, Issues (11, Carleton Gardens, Brecknock Road, London N19).

Zimet, S.G. (1976) *Print and prejudice*, Hodder & Stoughton.

Chapter 10

Dahl, R. (1982) *The BFG*, Cape.

Eggleston, J. *et al.* (1981) *Inservice teacher education in a multiracial society: report to the D.E.S.*, University of Keele.

Giles, R. and Cherrington, D. (1981), in M. Craft, *Teaching in a multicultural Society*, Falmer.

Jones, G. and Street-Porter, R. (1983) Antiracist teaching and teacher education, in *Multicultural Teaching*, vol. 1 no. 3.

Further reading

This lists only those books and articles dealing with bias in books and the media at a general level. Specific curriculum areas, e.g. the writings of Dawn Gill and David Hicks on Geography and Ann Marie Davies and Ann Hedge on History, are referred to in some depth in Chapter 5 and listed in the Citation Index.

Recommended reading on issues of racism and of sexism in schools and society can be found in the two Resources Guides described in the opening paragraph to the List of Organizations.

Adams, C. and Laurikietis, R. (1976) *The gender trap: a closer look at sex roles*. bk. 3, *Messages and images*.

Buckingham, D. (1983) 'Positive images?' in *Multicultural Teaching* vol. 2 no. 1.

Burgess, C. (1981) 'Counteracting stereotyping in the primary school' in *Dragon's Teeth* vol. 3, no. 2.

Davies, A. and Hedge, A. (forthcoming 1985) *Racism in print* Writers and Readers.

Dixon, B. (1977) *Catching them young* vol. 1: *Sex, race and class in children's fiction*, Pluto.

Foster, M. (1979) 'Do children have views about stereotyping?' in *Dragon's Teeth* vol. 1 no. 2.

Gill, D. (1983) 'Anti-racist teaching through Geography' in *Contemporary Issues in Geography Education* vol. 1 no. 1.

Glastonbury, M. (1982) 'What books tell girls' in *English Magazine* no. 9.

Goodall, P. (1982) 'Children's books: a feminist view' in *Schooling and Culture* no. 10.

Hicks, D. (1980) *Images of the world; an introduction to bias in teaching materials*, University of London Institute of Education.

Husband, C. (ed.) (1975) *White media and black Britain: a critical look at the role of the media in race relations today*, Arrow.

Knight, C. (1983) 'The evaluation of reading schemes for use in the

Further reading

multicultural classroom' in *Multicultural Teaching* vol. 2 no. 1.

Preiswerk, R. (ed.) (1980) *The slant of the pen; racism in children's books*, World Council of Churches.

Stinton, J. (ed.) (1979) *Racism and sexism in children's books*, Writers and Readers.

Stones, R. (1983) *'Pour out the cocoa, Janet'; sexism in children's books.* York, Longmans Resources Unit for Schools Council.

Verma, G. (1981) *A feasibility study of books and ethnic minorities*, Bradford University.

Women in History Group, ILEA (1983) 'Sexism in learning materials', in *Contemporary Issues in Geography and Education* vol. 1 no. 1. It is set in context by the article immediately preceding it: 'Sexim and racism: parallel experiences' by F. Slater.

Worrall, M. (1978) 'Multiracial Britain and the Third World: tensions and approaches in the classroom' in *New Era* vol. 59 no. 2.

Wright, D. (1983) 'They have no need of transport' in *Contemporary Issues in Georgraphy Education* vol. 1 no. 1.

158

List of organizations

Organizations referred to in the text. Fuller lists of relevant organizations, with brief accounts of the functions, services and publications of each, are:

The Anti-sexist resource guide compiled by Sue Adler and Annie Cornbleet for the Inner London Education Authority, ILEA 1984.

Resources for a multicultural society: an introduction 1982 – by Gillian Klein for Schools Council. 2nd revised edn 1984, York, Longmans Resources Unit.

Afro Caribbean Education Research (ACER) Wyvil School, Wyvil Road, London SW8.

All Faiths for One Race (AFFOR) 173, Lozells Road, Lozells, Birmingham B19 1RN.

All London Teachers Against Racism and Facism (ALTARF) Room 216, Panther House, Mount Pleasant, London WC1.

Assistant Masters and Mistresses Association (AMMA) 29, Gordon Square, London WC1.

Caribbean Teachers' Association, 8, Camberwell Green, London, SE5.

Campaign to Impede Sex Stereotyping in the Young (CISSY) 177, Gleneldon Road, London, SW16.

Catholic Commission for Racial Justice, 1, Amwell Street, London EC1.

Centre for World Development Education (CWDE) 128, Buckingham Palace Road, London SW1.

Commission for Racial Equality (CRE) Elliott House, Allington Street, London SE1.

Commonwealth Institute, Kensington High Street, London W8.

Community and Race Relations Unit of the British Council of Churches (CRRU) 2, Eaton Gate, London SW1.

Council on Interracial Books for Children (CIBC) 1841 Broadway, New York, NY 10023.

Equal Opportunities Commission (EOC) Overseas House, Quay Street, Manchester M3.

List of organizations

Fawcett Library, City of London Polytechnic, Old Castle Street, London E1.

Harmony, 22, St Mary's Road, Maire, near Glastonbury, Somerset.

ILEA Centre for Anti-Racist Education, Mawbey School, Coopers Road, London SE1.

ILEA English Centre, Ebury Bridge, Sutherland Street, London SW1.

ILEA Publications, 275, Kennington Lane, London SE11.

Institute of Race Relations, 2–6 Leeke St., Kings Cross Road, WC1X 9HS

Letterbox Library, Children's Book Cooperative (Booksellers) 42, Navick Road, London E5.

Library Association, 7 Ridgmount Street, London WC1.

National Association for Multiracial Education (NAME) P.O. Box 9, Walsall, West Midlands.

National Association for the Teaching of English, (NATE), 'Fernligh', 10b, Thornhill Road, Edgerton, Huddersfield.

National Book League, 45, East Hill, London SE18.

National Council for Mother Tongue Teaching (NCMTT) 4, Rutland Terrace, Stamford, Lincs.

National Union of Teachers (NUT) Hamilton House, Mabledon Place, London WC1.

New Beacon Books (Bookshop), 76, Stroud Green, London N4.

Oxfam Youth and Education Department, 274, Banbury Road, Oxford OX2.

Parents and Children and Teachers (PACT) Information on local branches from: PACT, Hackney Teachers' Centre, Pitfield Street, London E1.

Runnymede Trust, 37a, Gray's Inn Road, London WC1.

Shakti Bookhouse (Bookshop), 46, High Street, Southall, Middlesex.

Sisterwrite (Bookshop) 190, Upper Street, London, N1.

Soma Books (Bookshop) 38, Kennington Lane, London SE11 and at Commonwealth Institute.

Third World Publications (Bookshop) 151 Stratford Road, Birmingham B11 1RD.

United Kingdom Reading Association (UKRA) c/o Edge Hill College, St Helen's Road, Ormskirk, Lancs.

Walter Rodney (Bookshop) 5a, Chignell Place, Ealing, London W13.

Working Group against Racism in Children's Resources. (Contact person: Jane Lane at CRE, Elliott House, Allington Street, London SW1).

World Studies 8–13 Project. Centre for Peace Studies, St. Martin's College, Lancaster, LA1 3JD.

Author and citation index

ACER – Afro-Caribbean Education Resource Project, 26, 102, 159
Adams, Carol, 34, 37, 57
Aesop, 53
AFFOR, 82, 131, 159
Agard, John, 7
Ahlberg, A, 80–1
Ajegbo, K., 10
Alcott, Louisa May, 5, 45
Alexander, Ziggy, 21, 63, 94
ALTARF – All London Teachers Against Racism and Facism, 14, 17, 116, 159
Armstrong, W., 2
Ash, Ranjana, 137
Ashley, Bernard, 49
Augier, F.R., 65

Bahree, Patricia, 84
Banfield, Beryl, 4, 16, 46
Bannerman, Helen (*Little Black Sambo*), 15, 29, 79, 137
Bardell, G., 87
Bayfield, Tony, 2, 4, 98
BEANS Series, 32, 71–2, 134
Beier, Ulli, 53
Bennett, Olivia, 72, 138
Bernheim, Marc, 7, 31
Berry, James, 137
Beswick, Norman, 120, 146
Bethell, Andrew, 116
Bettleheim, Bruno, 11
Bishop, Claire, 55
Black Ink Collective, 103, 136, 159
Brandreth, G., 41, 113

British Council of Churches, 82, 86 (CRRU 159)
Bruce, R., 84
Buckingham, David, 34, 111 ff
BUF: Bilingual Under Fives Project (ILEA), 103
Bullock Report, 108
Burgess, Celia, 37
Butler, R., 85

Carr, Frank, 83
Carrington, B., 93
Ceserani, G., 62
Children's Book Bulletin, 17, 23, 66, 129
Claire, Hilary, 73
Coard, Bernard, 15
Colbert, J.H., 32
Commission for Racial Equality (CRE), 98, 101, 159
Coolidge, Susan, 5
Cox, J., 47
Craft, Alma, 87
Craft, Maurice, 144
Crawford, S., 57–8
Curtis, A., 59

Dahl, R., 117, 143
Davidson, Basil, 60, 73
Davies, Ann Marie, 17, 58, 64ff
Defoe, Daniel, 37, 44
de la Mare, W., 4, 50, 101
Dewjee, Audrey, 21, 63, 94
Dhondy, Farrukh, 5, 49, 81, 99, 112
Dickinson, Peter, 48
Dixon, Bob, 16, 128

Author and citation index

Educational Publishers Council, 137
Edwards, Viv, 101
Eggleston, John (S.J.), 93, 99, 144
Elkin, Judith, 20, 128
Explore-a-Story, 54
Explorers, 62, 63

Fawcett Library, 119, 131, 160
File, Nigel, 63, 94
Fisher, H.A.L., 92
Fisher, Simon, 2, 74
Fitzhugh, Louise, 2
Fletcher, H., 86
Floyd, L., 78
Foster, Marina, 97
Fox, Paula, 2, 134

Garfield, L., 48
Garvie, E., 96
Gatland, K., 88
Gen, 136, 155
Gilbert, Martin C., 98
Giles, Ray, 144
Gill, Dawn, 16, 58, 98
Gilroy, Beryl, 81
Glastonbury, Marion, 16, 28, 53, 129
Gombrich, E.H., 75
Goodall, Phil, 10, 124
Green, Peter, 97
Groves, P., 81
Gundara, Jagdish, 21
Gundara, Jaswinder, 21
Guy, Rosa, 2

Harmony, 11
Heapy, R., 79
Heaslip, Peter, 138
Hedge, A., 17, 58, 64ff
Hemmings, Ray, 87, 100
Hicks, David (D.W.), 2, 17, 18, 57, 69ff
    73–4, 114
Hill, Janet, 11, 19
Home Affairs Committee, 16, 108
Honeyford, Ray, 97
How they live now (series), 71
Hum Gar Chan, 66
Huntley, Accabre, 102

Illustrated London News, 62
Inner London Education Authority
    (ILEA), 15, 17, 19, 21, 59, 101, 103,
    115, 130, 133, 136, 144

Institute of Race Relations, 64, 131, 160
Interracial Books for Children, 18, 129

Janson, H.W., 75
Jones, Crispin, 17, 21, 144
Jones, Toekey, 137

Kaye, Geraldine, 46
Klein, Gillian, 17, 22, 131
Knight, Cynthia, 81
Kuya, Dorothy, 16, 25, 33

Lai Po Kan, 66
Language Diversity Project, 101–2
Larrabeti, Michael de, 112
Lashley, Jennie, 47
Laurokietis, Rae, 34, 37, 57
Lawton, Clive, 98
Lee, H., 2
Linguistic Minorities Project, 103
Lurie, Alison, 37, 55

MacDonald 'Countries', 67–8
McIver, A., 61
Mackay, 37
Manning, Rev. Basil, 41–2
Meek, Margaret, 11, 23
Milner, David, 14, 15, 18, 25, 34
Mitter, Swasti, 69
Multicultural Educational Abstracts, 119
Multicultural Teaching, 23, 129, 144–5,
    156

NAME – National Association for
    Multiracial Education (from 1985
    National Movement Against Racism
    in Education), 19, 95, 98, 101, 160
NATE – National Association for the
    Teaching of English, 95, 160
National Council for Mother Tongue
    Teaching, 103, 160
Needle, Jan, 51, 134

O&B Maths Bank II, 88
Oxford Junior Book on Africa, 59
Oxford Junior Companion to Music, 78

Perambulavil, V., 78
Perkins, T., 34
Petersen, P., 71
Power, Christopher, 63, 94
Preiswerk, Roy, 4, 5, 17, 30, 82, 85

Price, Willard, 45

Reading On; Red Book One, 1
Resch, Barbara, 53
Richardson, Robin, 73
Rose, Steven, 6, 88ff
Rosen, Harold, 102
Ross, Alistair, 87
Rosten, Leo, 54
Ruddell, David, 85
Ruhr, M., 98

Scarman Report, 108
Schools Council, 8, 96, 98, 103
Scope, 79
Seacole, Mary, 63, 94
Searle, Chris, 115
Share-a-Story, 54
Shawcroft, Christine, 123
Shepherd, Francis, 77
Shyllon, F., 63
Sivanandan, A., 4, 62
Solomon, Joan, 72
Spender, Dale, 27
Stanley, F., 40
Steel, F.A., 54
Stone, Maureen, 99
Stones, Rosemary, 17, 28, 37, 48, 57,
    127, 139
Storm, Michael, 36
*Studies in Design Education Craft and
    Technology*, 97

Tames, Richard, 84
Tate, Joan, 47, 79–80
Taylor, Theodore, 2, 37
Thewlis, J., 61
Townsend, P., 61
Trudgill, Peter, 101
Twain, Mark, 45

Wallace, J., 45
Wallman, Sandra, 34
Walvin, James, 63
Warwick, Roger, 121
Whitehead, Frank, 14
Willey, Richard, 17
Williams, J., 55
Williams, Ursula Moray, 51
Wood, A., 11
Wood, E., 93
Woodcock, R., 62
World of Musical Instruments, 78
World Studies Project, 73
Worrall, Mary, 8, 17
Wright, David, 58, 67
Wright, J.A., 103

Young, Ed., 40

Zaslavsky, Claudia, 87
Zeiris, M., 66
Zimet, Sara Goodman, 16, 124

Subject index

Africa, 31, 59–62, 64ff, 87
Alternative Publishers, 126, 136ff
Anti-semitism, 3, 4, 35, 98
Art, 77ff
Assemblies, 82ff

Bibliographies, 127–8
Bilingualism, 100, 103–4
Biological determinism, 88–90
Black consciousness, 15

Cannibals, 40, 80, 88
Censorship, 33, 60, 123ff, 134–5
Challenging bias, 113ff, 120ff
Charity, 85–6
Children's responses to bias, 23, 114, 117, 120
Class prejudice, 5
Classroom texts, 112ff
Colonialism, 59ff
Comic books, 47
Community languages, 100, 103–4, 106, 111, 113
Complaints about bias, 116, 132
Craft Design and Technology, 86, 93, 96
Creative freedom, 27
Criteria for selecting books, 17ff, 22ff, 109, 124
Curriculum, *see also* individual curriculum areas, 75ff, 92ff, 125, 135
  hidden curriculum, 75, 92ff

Darwin, Evolutionary theory, 89
Demystifying print, 25, 114ff
Development Education, 57ff

'Development' and 'Underdevelopment', 69
Dewey Decimal Classification, 105ff
Dialect, 100ff, 115

Early Reading, 24, 115
Encyclopedias, 91
English, 101ff; as a Second Language, 95, 100
Ethnocentricism, 59, 67, 92
Evaluation Skills, 19
Examinations, 97
Exhibitions, 127, 129ff
Explorers, 62–3, 135

Family Co-operation in Early Literacy Project, 11
Fiction, 22, 44ff
Folktales, 53ff

Geography, 57ff, 114ff
Golliwogs, 40ff, 113
Guidance in book selection, 124, 130–1, 133ff, 138

Hidden curriculum, 75
History, 33, 57ff
Home Economics, 96

Identification, 6, 13
Identity, 35
Illustrations, 7, 47, 55, 66–7, 81, 88, 116–17, 135;
  self-portraits, 14
India, 65, 67, 69, 87

Initial Literacy, 24
Inner London Education Authority, 21;
  see also Author and Citation Index
In-service Training, 109–10
Intellectual freedom, 122, 124

Jokes, 39–40, 87–8
Journals, 23, 129

Language, 22, 27, 32, 61, 67, 100ff;
  primers, 78
Liberation Struggles, 65
Libraries, 20, 93, 104ff, 110, 115, 118ff,
  124, 131ff
Linguistic diversity, 101

Maps, 68
Mathematics, 86, 100
Mother Tongue, 100, 103–4, 135, 138
Multicultural Resource Centres, 130–1
Music, 7ff, 99

NAME, 19, 95, 101, 160

Omission, 30ff, 67, 76, 86ff

PACT, 11
Parental Involvement, 11, 104
Periodicals, 23, 129
Poverty, 114
Primers, 78
Protests about Bias, 116, 132, 145
Psychometry, 89
Publishers, 117;
  Alternative, 126, 136;
  Catalogues, 126

Race Relations in the curriculum, 116
Racist Bias, 4, 25ff, 30ff, 44ff, 84ff, 92ff
Reading research, 14
Reading Schemes, 7, 15, 81ff
Religious Education, 82ff
Remedial Readers, 47, 79, 113
Reviews, 21, 23, 127
Role stereotyping, 36ff

School libraries, 20, 93, 104ff, 110, 115,
  118ff, 132–3
Schools Council, 96, 98, 103
Science, 86, 88ff
Selection guidance, 124, 130–1, 133ff,
  138
Selection of materials, 17ff, 22ff, 120,
  123ff, 131ff
Self portraits, 14
Sexism, 6, 27, 33, 36, 47–8, 53–5, 57, 86,
  96
Slavery, 59, 64–6
Specialist bookshops, 129–30, 131–7
Sport, 93
Statistics, 68
Stereotyping, 4, 7, 18, 30, 34ff, 47, 96,
  111ff
Study Skills, 120ff
Support Services, Public Library, 20,
  131, 134–5

Teaching methodology, 102, 112ff, 120ff
Timetabling, 99ff, 103

World religions, 83ff
World Studies, 57ff
World Studies Project, 36, 114